From the
GASSER COLLECTION

Given by the friends of
WILLIAM D. GASSER, CPA

In honor of his being named
Professor
and
Outstanding Teacher for 1971
June 24, 1971

The Gasser Collection

Wallace Memorial Library
Rochester Institute of Technology

INTERNATIONAL ACCOUNTING STANDARDS

A PRACTICAL GUIDE
SECOND EDITION

INTERNATIONAL ACCOUNTING STANDARDS

A PRACTICAL GUIDE
SECOND EDITION

HENNIE VAN GREUNING

MARIUS KOEN

THE WORLD BANK

First Edition 1999
Second Edition 2001
Third Edition 2002

Hennie van Greuning is Advisor – Treasury Operations, the World Bank.
Marius Koen is Senior Financial Management Specialist, Africa Region, the World Bank.

Typesetting by Louise Oberholster.

ISBN 0-8213-4999-6

Library of Congress Cataloging-in-Publication data has been applied for.

CONTENTS

PREFACE

In response to the global financial crisis in 1998, several international organizations, including the World Bank and the International Monetary Fund, launched a cooperative initiative to strengthen the global financial architecture. Although International Accounting Standards (IASs) have been in existence for many years, this initiative has given them an added importance. In particular, they help to promote transparency in financial reporting and the harmonization of standards needed to support increasingly globalized financial markets.

The World Bank urges national regulators to accept the IASs in preference to the development of country-specific practices due to their broad international acceptance and flexibility in incorporating a wide range of international best practices. The Bank also accepts IASs as a basis for the preparation of the financial statements it receives from borrowers on the use of Bank loans and credits. In the last year, IASs received a further boost following endorsement by the International Organization of Securities Commission (IOSCO) and their adoption by the European Union.

The World Bank has supported the recent process of restructuring the International Accounting Standards Committee (IASC) to make it a more representative and effective global regulatory body. We are particularly keen that developing countries and those in transition have a voice in the standard-setting process and that IASs are disseminated as widely as possible. This text, now in its second edition and being translated into several languages, is an important contribution to expanding awareness and understanding of IASs around the world, with it easy-to-read summaries of each standard and case studies that illustrate accounting treatments and disclosure requirements. We are very grateful to its authors, Hennie van Greuning and Marius Koen.

Paul Bermingham
Chairman: Financial Management Sector Board
World Bank
Washington D.C. USA
January 8, 2001

INTRODUCTION

When this publication was developed, a conscious decision was made to focus on the needs of senior executives in the private and public sectors who do not have a strong accounting background. This publication summarizes each International Accounting Standard so that managers and executives can obtain a broad and basic understanding of the key issues within a minimum time frame.

In addition to the short summaries, each chapter contains a simple case study that emphasizes the practical application of some key concepts in a particular standard. The non-technical reader is therefore provided with the tools to participate in an informed manner in discussions relating to the appropriateness or application of a standard in a given situation. The reader can also evaluate the effect that the application of the principles of a given accounting standard will have on the financial results and position of a division or an entire enterprise.

HOW TO USE THIS PUBLICATION

The authors have created a template to facilitate discussion of each standard.
1. **Problems addressed** identifies the main objectives and the key issues of the standard.
2. **Scope of the standard** identifies the specific transactions and events covered by a standard. In certain instances, compliance to the requirements of a standard is limited to a specified range of enterprises.
3. **Accounting treatment** lists the specific accounting principles, bases, conventions, rules, and practices that should be adopted by an enterprise for compliance with a particular standard.
4. **Disclosure** describes the manner in which the financial and non-financial items should be presented in the financial statements as well as aspects that should be disclosed in these financial statements.

The authors hope that managers in the client countries of the World Bank will find this format useful in establishing accounting terminology, especially where certain terms are still in the exploratory stage. Feedback in this regard is welcome.

CONTENT

All of the accounting standards issued by the International Accounting Standards Committee (IASC) as well as interpretations issued by the Standards Interpretations Committee (SIC) until 31 December 2000 are included in this publication.

ACKNOWLEDGMENT

The authors gratefully acknowledge the financial support provided by a PHRD-grant for the preparation of an accounting development component of an Institutional Development Loan to Russia for the initial development of this publication.

CHAPTER 1

TRANSPARENCY IN FINANCIAL STATEMENTS

The provision of transparent and useful information on market participants and their transactions is essential for an orderly and efficient market, and it is one of the most important preconditions for imposing market discipline. Left to themselves, markets may not generate sufficient levels of disclosure. Market forces would normally balance the marginal benefits and marginal costs of additional information disclosure and the end result may not be what the market participants really need.

Financial and capital market liberalization trends of the 1980s, which brought increasing volatility in financial markets, increased the need for information as a means to ensure financial stability. In the 1990s, as financial and capital market liberalization increased, there has been mounting pressure for the provision of useful information in both the financial and private sectors; minimum disclosure requirements now dictate the quality and quantity of information that must be provided to the market participants and to the general public. Because the provision of information is essential to promote the stability of the markets, regulatory authorities also view the **quality of information** as a high priority. Once the quality of information required by market participants and regulatory authorities is improved, entities would do well to improve their own internal information systems so as to develop a reputation for providing good quality information.

The public disclosure of information is predicated on the existence of good accounting standards and adequate disclosure methodology. This public disclosure normally involves publication of relevant qualitative and quantitative information in annual financial reports, which are often supplemented by interim financial statements and other relevant information. The provision of information involves cost; therefore, when determining disclosure requirements, its usefulness for the public must be evaluated against the cost to be borne by the enterprise.

The timing of disclosure is also important. Disclosure of negative information to a public not yet sufficiently sophisticated to interpret the information may damage the enterprise in question. When information is of inadequate quality and/or the users are not deemed capable to properly interpret the information, public disclosure requirements should be carefully phased in and progressively tightened. In the long run, a full disclosure regime is beneficial, even if some problems are experienced in the short term, because the cost to the financial system of not being transparent is ultimately higher than the cost of being transparent.

TRANSPARENCY AND ACCOUNTABILITY

Transparency refers to the principle of creating an environment where information on existing conditions, decisions, and actions are made accessible, visible, and understandable to all market participants. **Disclosure** refers to the process and methodology of providing the information and making policy decisions known through timely dissemination and openness. **Accountability** refers to the need for market participants, including the authorities, to justify their actions and policies and accept responsibility for their decisions and results.

Transparency is necessary for the concept of accountability to take hold amongst the three major groups of market participants: borrowers and lenders, issuers and investors, as well as national authorities and international financial institutions.

Transparency and accountability have become strongly debated topics in discussions of economic policy over the past decade. Policymakers had become accustomed to secrecy. Secrecy was viewed as a necessary ingredient for the exercise of power, with an added benefit of hiding the incompetence of policymakers. However, secrecy also prevents policies from having their desired effects. The changed world economy and financial flows, which brought the increasing internationalization and interdependence, have put the openness issue at the forefront of economic policy making. There is a growing recognition of national governments, including central banks, that transparency (i.e., the openness of policy) improves the predictability and, hence, the efficiency of policy decisions. Transparency forces institutions to face up to the reality of a situation and makes officials more responsible, especially if they know they will have to justify their views, decisions, and actions afterwards. Timely policy adjustments are therefore encouraged.

In part, the case for greater transparency and accountability rests on the need for private sector agents to understand and accept policy decisions that will affect their behavior. Greater transparency improves the economic decisions made by other agents in the economy. Transparency is also a means of fostering accountability, internal discipline, and better governance. Transparency and accountability improve the quality of decision making in policy-making institutions (whose activities should normally be required to be transparent) as well as in institutions whose own decisions depend on understanding and predicting the future decisions of policy-making institutions. If actions and decisions are visible and understandable, monitoring costs are lowered. The general public will be better able to monitor public sector institutions; shareholders and employees to monitor corporate management; creditors to monitor borrowers, and depositors to monitor banks. Therefore, poor decisions will not go unnoticed or unquestioned.

Transparency and accountability are mutually reinforcing. Transparency enhances accountability by facilitating monitoring, and accountability enhances transparency by providing an incentive for agents to ensure that the reasons for their actions are properly disseminated and understood. Together, transparency and accountability will:

- impose a discipline that improves the quality of decision making in the public sector, and
- lead to more efficient policy by improving the private sector's understanding of how policy-makers may react to various events in the future.

WHAT TRANSPARENCY CANNOT ENSURE: Transparency and accountability are not ends in themselves. They are designed to assist in increasing economic performance and may improve the working of the international financial markets by enhancing the quality of decision-making and risk management of all market participants, including official authorities. But they are not a panacea. In particular, transparency does not change the nature or risks inherent in financial systems. It may not prevent financial crises, but may moderate market participants' response to bad news. Transparency then helps market participants to anticipate and qualify bad news and thereby lessens the probability of panic and contagion.

CONSTRAINTS ON TRANSPARENCY: One must also note that there is a dichotomy between transparency and confidentiality. The release of proprietary information may give competitors an unfair advantage, a fact that deters market participants from full disclosure. Similarly, monitoring bodies frequently obtain confidential information from entities. The release of such information may have significant market implications. Under such circumstances, enterprises may be reluctant to provide sensitive information without the condition of client confidentiality. However, unilateral transparency and full disclosure contributes to a regime of transparency, which will ultimately benefits all market participants, even if in the short-term, a transition to such a regime creates discomfort for individual entities.

TRANSPARENCY IN FINANCIAL STATEMENTS

The objective of financial statements is to provide information about the financial position **(balance sheet)**, performance **(income statement)**, and changes in financial position **(cash flow statement)** of an entity. The transparency of financial statements is secured through full disclosure and by providing fair presentation of useful information necessary for making economic decisions to a wide range of users. In the context of public disclosure, financial statements should be easy to interpret. While more information is better than less, the provision of information is costly. Therefore, the net benefits of providing more transparency should be carefully evaluated.

The adoption of internationally accepted accounting standards is a necessary measure to facilitate transparency and proper interpretation of financial statements. The International Accounting Standards Committee (IASC) developed a *Framework for the Preparation and Presentation of Financial Statements*, published in 1989. This framework:

- **Lists concepts** underlying the preparation and presentation of financial statements to external users;

- **Guides** standards-setters in developing accounting standards, and

- **Assists** preparers, auditors, and users in interpreting International Accounting Standards (IAS) and dealing with issues not yet covered by such standards.

According to the international standards, financial statements are normally prepared assuming that the enterprise will continue to operate as **a going concern** and that events are recorded on an **accrual basis**, that is, the effects of transactions and other events are recognized when they occur. They are then reported in the financial statements of the periods to which they relate.

Qualitative characteristics are those attributes that make the information provided in financial statements **useful** to its users. If comprehensive useful information is absent, even managers may not be aware of the true financial condition of their enterprise, other key players may be misled, and this may prevent market disciplines from working. The application of the principal qualitative characteristics and of appropriate accounting standards normally results in financial statements that give a true and fair presentation.

The key qualitative characteristics are:

- **Relevance:** Information is relevant when it influences the economic decisions of users by helping them evaluate past, present, and future events or to confirm/correct their past evaluations. The relevance of information is affected by its nature and materiality (which is always the threshold for relevance). Information overload, on the other hand, can obfuscate information, making it hard to sift through the relevant nuggets and making interpretation difficult.

- **Reliability:** Information should be free from material errors and bias. The key aspects of reliability are faithful representation, priority of substance over form, neutrality, prudence, and completeness.

- **Comparability:** Information should be presented in a consistent manner over time and consistent between entities to enable users to make significant comparisons.

- **Understandability:** Information should be readily understandable by users who are expected to have a reasonable knowledge of business, economics and accounting and a willingness to study the information with reasonable diligence.

The process of producing useful information includes a number of decision points, which may constrain the amount of information provided. These include:

- **Timeliness:** A delay in reporting may improve reliability at the cost of relevance.

- **Benefit vs. Cost:** Benefits derived from information should normally exceed the cost of providing it.

- **Balancing of Qualitative Characteristics:** To meet the objectives of financial statements and make them adequate for a particular environment, providers of information must achieve an appropriate balance among qualitative characteristics.

In the context of fair presentation, it is better to disclose no information than to disclose misleading information. It is therefore not surprising that, when an enterprise does not comply with specific disclosure requirements, International Accounting Standards would normally require full disclosure of the fact and the reasons for non-compliance. Figure 1 shows how transparency is secured through the IAS framework.

FIGURE 1

TRANSPARENCY IN FINANCIAL STATEMENTS

OBJECTIVE OF FINANCIAL STATEMENTS
  To provide a fair presentation of:
  • Financial position
  • Financial performance
  • Cash flows

TRANSPARENCY AND FAIR PRESENTATION
  • Fair presentation achieved through providing useful information (full disclosure)
    which would secure transparency
  • Fair presentation equates Transparency

SECONDARY OBJECTIVE OF FINANCIAL STATEMENTS
  To secure **transparency** through a fair presentation of **useful** information (full disclosure)
  for decision making purposes

ATTRIBUTES OF USEFUL INFORMATION
  • Relevance   **Constraints**
    = Nature
    = Materiality
  • Reliability
    = Faithful representation   Timeliness
    = Substance over form
    = Neutrality   Benefit vs. Cost
    = Prudence
    = Completeness   Balancing the qualitative characteristics
  • Comparability
  • Understandability

UNDERLYING ASSUMPTIONS	
Accrual basis	Going concern

CHAPTER 2

FRAMEWORK FOR THE PREPARATION AND PRESENTATION OF FINANCIAL STATEMENTS

2.1 PROBLEMS ADDRESSED

Accounting standards should be prepared within an acceptable coherent framework of fundamental principles. The IASC's *Framework for the Preparation and Presentation of Financial Statements* was published in 1989. This framework:
- Introduces concepts underlying the preparation and presentation of financial statements.
- Guides standard-setters in developing accounting standards.
- Assists preparers, auditors, and users in interpreting the IAS and in dealing with issues not yet covered by the IAS.

2.2 SCOPE OF THE FRAMEWORK

The framework is **not** a standard. The framework incorporates:
- Objectives of financial statements (see paragraph 2.3.1).
- Qualitative characteristics of financial statements (see paragraph 2.3.4).
- Elements of financial statements (see paragraphs 2.3.6 & 2.3.7).
- Concepts of capital and capital maintenance (see paragraph 2.3.10).

2.3 ACCOUNTING CONCEPTS

2.3.1 The objective of financial statements is to provide information about the **financial position** (balance sheet), **performance** (income statement), and **changes in financial position** (cash flow statement) of an enterprise that is useful to a wide range of users in making economic decisions.

2.3.2 Fair presentation is achieved through the provision of useful information (full disclosure) in the financial statements, whereby **transparency** is secured. If one assumes that fair presentation is equivalent to transparency, a secondary objective of financial statements can be developed: **to secure transparency through full disclosure and provide a fair presentation of useful information for decision making purposes.**

2.3.3 The following are the underlying assumptions to financial statements:
- **Accrual basis:** Effects of transactions and other events are recognized when they occur (not when the cash flows). These are recorded and reported in the financial statements of the periods to which they relate.
- **Going concern concept:** It is assumed that the entity will continue to operate for the foreseeable future.

2.3.4 Qualitative characteristics are the attributes that make the information provided in financial statements **useful** to users.
- **Relevance:** Relevant information influences the economic decisions of users, helping them to evaluate past, present, and future events or to confirm/correct their past evaluations. The relevance of information is affected by its nature and materiality.
- **Reliability:** Reliable information is free from material error and bias and it is guided by:
  - Faithful representation.
  - Substance over form.
  - Neutrality.

- ▪ Prudence.
- ▪ Completeness.
- **Comparability:** Information should be presented consistently over time and consistently between enterprises so that users can make significant comparisons.
- **Understandability:** Information should be readily understandable by users who have a basic knowledge of business, economics, and accounting, and a willingness to study.

2.3.5 The following are constraints on providing relevant and reliable information:
- **Timeliness:** Undue delay in reporting may result in loss of relevance but improve reliability.
- **Benefit vs. Cost:** Benefits derived from information should exceed the cost of providing it.
- **Balancing qualitative characteristics:** The aim is to achieve a balance among characteristics in order to meet the objective of financial statements.

The application of the principal qualitative characteristics and the appropriate accounting standards normally results in financial statements that give **a true and fair view/fair presentation.**

2.3.6 The following elements of financial statements are directly related to the measurement of the **financial position:**
- **Assets:** Resources controlled by the enterprise as a result of past events and from which future economic benefits are expected to flow to the enterprise.
- **Liabilities:** Present obligations of an enterprise arising from past events, the settlement of which is expected to result in an outflow from the enterprise of economic benefits.
- **Equity:** Assets less liabilities (commonly known as shareholders' funds).

2.3.7 The following elements of financial statements are directly related to the measurement of **performance:**
- **Income:** Increases in economic benefits in the form of inflows or enhancements of assets, or decreases of liabilities that result in an increase in equity (other than increases resulting from contributions by owners). Income embraces revenue and gains.
- **Expenses:** Decreases in economic benefits in the form of outflows or depletion of assets, or incurrences of liabilities that result in decreases in equity (other than decreases because of distributions to owners).

2.3.8 An element should be recognized in the financial statements if:
- It is **probable** that any future economic benefit associated with the item will flow to or from the enterprise; and
- The item has a cost or value that can be **measured with reliability**.

2.3.9 The following bases are used to measure elements of financial statements:
- Historical cost.
- Current cost.
- Realizable (settlement) value.
- Present value

2.3.10 Concepts of capital and capital maintenance include:
- **Financial capital:** Capital is synonymous with net assets/equity; it is defined in terms of nominal monetary units. Profit represents the increase in nominal money capital over the period.
- **Physical capital:** Capital is regarded as the operating capability; it is defined in terms of the productive capacity. Profit represents the increase in productive capacity over the period.

CASE STUDY

FRAMEWORK FOR THE PREPARATION AND PRESENTATION OF FINANCIAL STATEMENTS

Chemco Inc. is engaged in the production of chemical products and selling them locally. The corporation wishes to extend its market and export some of its products to overseas countries.

It has come to the attention of the financial director that compliance with international environmental requirements is a significant precondition if it wishes to sell products overseas. Although the corporation has, during the past, put in place a series of environmental policies, it is clear that it is also common practice to have an environmental audit done from time to time which will cost approximately $120,000. The audit will encompass the following:
- Full review of all environmental policy directives.
- Detailed analysis of compliance with these directives.
- Report containing in-depth recommendations of those physical and policy changes that would be necessary to meet international requirements.

The financial director of Chemco Inc. has suggested that the $120,000 be capitalized as an asset and then written off against the revenues generated from export activities so that the matching of income and expense will occur.

The costs associated with the environmental audit can possibly be deferred according to **the matching concept**. The application of the matching concept in terms of the Framework, however, does not allow the recognition of items in the balance sheet that do not conform to the definition of elements of the financial statements.

In order to recognize the costs of the audit as an asset, it should meet both the:
- definition of an asset, and
- recognition criteria for an asset

In order for the costs associated with the environmental audit to comply with the **definition of an asset** (see paragraph 2.3.6), the following should be valid:
(i)   The costs must be a resource under the control of Chemco Inc., being the actual costs incurred.
(ii)   The asset must arise from a past transaction or event, namely the audit.
(iii) The asset must be expected to give rise to a probable future economic benefit which will flow to the corporation, namely the revenue from export sales.

The requirements in terms of (i) and (ii) are being met. However, there are problems regarding requirement (iii). Chemco Inc. wishes to export their products. The wish only is not sufficient evidence to satisfy this requirement. The corporation cannot capitalize these costs due to the absence of fixed orders and detailed analyses of expected economic benefits.

In order to **recognize** the costs as an asset in the balance sheet, it has to comply with the recognition criteria (see paragraph 2.3.8), namely:
- The asset should have a cost that can be measured reliably.
- The expected inflow of future economic benefits must be probable.

In order to properly measure the carrying value of the asset, the corporation must be able to demonstrate that further costs will be incurred that would give rise to future benefits. However, the second requirement poses a problem because of insufficient evidence of the probable inflow of economic benefits and would therefore disqualify the costs a second time for capitalization as an asset.

CHAPTER 3

PRESENTATION OF FINANCIAL STATEMENTS (IAS 1)

3.1 PROBLEMS ADDRESSED

The objective of the standard is to prescribe the basis for presentation of general purpose financial statements to ensure comparability. It outlines:
- Overall considerations for presentation.
- Guidelines for their structure.
- Minimum content requirements.
- Guidance on compliance with the IAS.
- Guidance on departures from the IAS.

3.2 SCOPE OF THE STANDARD

This standard deals with the presentation of all **general purpose financial statements** prepared and presented in accordance with the IAS and which are not tailored to meet specific information needs of users. *SIC–2 provides guidance on the first time application of IASs.*

3.3 ACCOUNTING CONCEPTS

3.3.1 Financial statements should provide information about an enterprise's financial position, performance, and cash flows that is useful for economic decision making.

3.3.2 The board of directors and/or other governing body is responsible for the preparation and presentation of financial statements.

3.3.3 A complete set of financial statements includes:
- Balance Sheet.
- Income Statement.
- Changes in Equity Statement.
- Cash Flow Statement.
- Accounting Policies & Notes.

Entities are encouraged to furnish other related financial and nonfinancial information in addition to the financial statements.

3.3.4 Management should consider all of the following **overall considerations** regarding the presentation of financial statements:
- **Fair presentation**
  This is normally achieved by applying the IAS. Departure is allowed only if the application of an accounting standard would result in misleading financial statements.
- **Compliance with the IAS**
  The following aspects should be addressed:
  - Compliance with the IAS should be disclosed.
  - Compliance with **all** requirements of each standard is compulsory.
  - Disclosure is no excuse for inappropriate accounting treatments.
  - Premature compliance with an IAS is to be mentioned.
  - Any departure from an IAS that is necessary to achieve fair presentation should be disclosed in detail.

- **Accounting policies**
  Accounting policies that are applied should be those required by the IAS. An enterprise would develop its own **relevant** and **reliable** policies if no IAS exist *(SIC–18)*.

The following two considerations are the underlying assumptions of financial statements; for more information, see chapter 2.

- **Going concern**
  Financial statements should be presented on a going concern basis unless it is probable that an entity will be liquidated or cease trading. If not presented on going concern basis, disclose the fact and rationale for not using it. Uncertainties regarding going concern should be disclosed.
- **Accrual basis**
  Use the accrual basis for presentation except for the cash flow statement.
- **Consistency of presentation**
  The presentation and classification of items should be retained from one period to another unless a change would result in a more appropriate presentation, or a change was required by the IAS.
- **Materiality and Aggregation**
  Aggregation of immaterial items of a similar nature and function is allowed. Material items should not be aggregated.
- **Offsetting**
  Assets and liabilities should not be offset unless allowed by the IAS. However, immaterial gains, losses, and related expenses arising from similar transactions and events may be offset.
- **Comparative information**
  The following aspects are relevant:
  - Disclosure required for numerical information in respect of the previous period.
  - Relevant narrative and descriptive information to be included.
  - Reclassify comparatives when classification of items is amended; that is, disclose nature, amounts, and reason(s).

3.4 DISCLOSURE

3.4.1 Identification and period
- Financial statements should be distinguished from other information.
- Each component should be clearly identified.
- Prominently display:
  - Name of reporting enterprise.
  - Own or group statements.
  - Reporting date or period.
  - Reporting currency.
  - Level of precision.
- Report annually, at the very least.
- Statements to be issued timely (within 6 months of reporting date).

3.4.2 Balance sheet
Provide information about the financial position.
Current/Non-current distinction
- Enterprise may choose this classification for assets and liabilities.
- If not chosen, assets and liabilities should be presented in broad order of liquidity.
- Split amounts to be recovered or settled within and after 12 months.

Current assets

- Current assets include:
  - Assets expected to be realized — or held for sale or consumption — in the normal operating cycle.
  - Assets held primarily for trading or over the short-term and expected to be realized within 12 months.
  - Cash or cash equivalents not restricted in use.

Current liabilities

- Current liabilities include:
  - Liabilities expected to be settled in the normal operating cycle.
  - Liabilities due to be settled within 12 months.
- Long-term interest-bearing liabilities to be settled within 12 months may be classified as non-current if:
  - Original term greater than 12 months.
  - Intention to refinance obligation.
  - Intention supported by agreement.

Minimum information on the face of the balance sheet

Property, plant, and equipment	Minority interest	Non-current interest-bearing
Intangible assets	Cash and cash equivalents	liabilities
Financial assets	Trade and other payables	Trade and other receivables
Investments accounted	Tax liabilities	Issued capital
for by the equity method	Tax assets	Reserves
Inventories	Provisions	

Other information on the face or in notes

- Appropriate additional subclassifications.
- Amounts payable to and from:
  - Parent enterprise.
  - Fellow subsidiaries.
  - Associates.
  - Related parties.
- For each class of share capital:
  - Number of shares authorized.
  - Number of shares issued and fully paid.
  - Number of shares issued and not fully paid.
  - Par value per share, or that it has no par value.
  - Reconciliation of shares at beginning and end of year.
  - Rights, preferences, and restrictions.
  - Held by enterprise, subsidiaries, or associates.
  - Reserved for issue under options and sales contracts.
- Nature and purpose of each reserve.
  - Shareholders for dividend not formally approved for payment.
  - Amount of cumulative preference dividend not recognized.

3.4.3   Income statement

Provide information about performance.

Minimum information on the face of the income statement

Revenue	Tax expense
Results of operating activities	Profit or loss from ordinary activities
Finance costs	Extraordinary items
Share of profits/losses of associates	Minority interest
and joint ventures, being equity accounted	Net profit or loss for the period

Other information on the face or in notes

- Analysis of expenses based on **nature** or their **function** (see case study).
- If classified by function, disclose:
  - Depreciation charges for tangible assets
  - Amortization charges for intangible assets.
  - Staff costs.
- Dividends per share declared or proposed.

3.4.4 Changes in equity statement

Reflect information about the increase/decrease in net assets or wealth.

Minimum information on the face of the changes in equity statement

- Net profit/loss for the period.
- Income, expense, gain, or loss taken **directly** to equity.
- Effects of changes in accounting policy.
- Effects of correction of fundamental errors.

Other information on the face or in notes

- Capital transactions with owners and distributions to owners.
- Reconciliation of the balance of accumulated profit or loss at beginning and end of the year.
- Reconciliation of the carrying amount of each class of equity capital, share premium, and each reserve at beginning and end of the period.

3.4.5 Cash flow statement Refer to IAS 7 (Chapter 5).

3.4.6 Accounting Policies and Notes

Information about the following is provided:

- Basis of preparation and selected accounting policies.
- Information required by the IAS that is not on the face of financial statements.
- Additional information required for fair presentation.

Structure

- Presented in a systematic manner.
- Cross-reference items from the face of financial statements to the notes.

Presentation of accounting policies

- Measurement bases used in preparing financial statements.
- Each accounting policy used even if it is not covered by the existing IAS.

Other disclosures

- Domicile of the enterprise.
- Legal form of the enterprise.
- Country of incorporation.
- Registered office/business address.
- Nature of operations/principal activities.
- Name of the parent and ultimate parent.
- Average number of employees.

CASE STUDY

PRESENTATION OF FINANCIAL STATEMENTS

Elrali Inc. is a manufacturing enterprise. The following is a summary of the income and expenses for the year ending 31 March 20x7:

	$
Gross turnover	7,500,000
Cost of sales of finished goods	3,995,100
Materials used	910,100
Labor	1,200,000
Variable production overhead costs allocated	800,000
Fixed production overhead costs allocated	845,000
Packing material	310,000
Cost of finished goods manufactured	4,065,100
Opening inventories finished goods	70,000
Closing inventories finished goods	(140,000)
Distribution costs	718,800
Administrative expenses	929,100
Other operating expenses	587,100
Investment income	124,800
Rental income	17,000
Finance costs	234,000
Write-down of cost of materials to net realizable value	25,000
Over-recovery of fixed production overhead costs	41,000
Abnormal spillage of materials	15,000
Income tax expense	319,700
Extraordinary profit	43,100

Depreciation and amortization charges included in the fixed production overheads amounted to $418,000, and those included in administrative expenses amounted to $205,000. Total salaries and other staff costs included in administrative expenses amount to $689,300.

The following income statements could be prepared based on the two alternative classifications of income and expenses allowed by IAS 1 (see paragraph 3.4.3):

CASE STUDY

CONTINUED

PRESENTATION OF FINANCIAL STATEMENTS

ELRALI INC.
INCOME STATEMENT FOR THE YEAR ENDING 31 MARCH 20x7
Classification of expenses by function

	$
Revenue	7,500,000
Cost of sales **(Calculation a)**	(3,994,100)
Gross profit	3,505,900
Other operating income **(Calculation b)**	141,800
Distribution costs	(718,800)
Administrative expenses	(929,100)
Other operating expenses	(587,100)
Profit from operations	1,412,700
Finance costs	(234,000)
Profit before tax	1,178,700
Income tax expense	(319,700)
Profit after tax from ordinary activities	859,000
Extraordinary item	43,100
Net profit for the period	902,100

ELRALI INC.
INCOME STATEMENT FOR THE YEAR ENDING 31 MARCH 20x7
Classification of expenses by nature

	$
Revenue	7,500,000
Other operating income **(Calculation b)**	141,800
Changes in inventories of finished goods and work in progress	70,000
Work performed by the enterprise and capitalized **(Calculation c)**	1,186,000)
Raw material and consumables used **(Calculation d)**	(1,260,100)
Staff costs **(Calculation e)**	(1,889,300)
Depreciation and amortization expenses (418 + 205)	(623,000)
Other operating expenses **(Calculation f)**	(1,340,700)
Profit from operations	1,412,700
Finance costs	(234,000)
Profit before tax	1,178,700
Income tax expense	(319,700)
Profit after tax from ordinary activities	859,000
Extraordinary item	43,100
Net profit for the period	902,100

CASE STUDY

CONTINUED

PRESENTATION OF FINANCIAL STATEMENTS

CALCULATIONS

		$
a.	**Cost of sales**	
	Amount given	3,995,100
	Write-down to net realizable value	25,000
	Over-recovery of fixed production overheads	(41,000)
	Abnormal materials spillage	15,000
		3,994,100
b.	**Other operating income**	
	Investment income	124,800
	Rental income	17,000
		141,800
c.	**Work performed and capitalized**	
	Variable production overheads	800,000
	Fixed production overheads (845 – 41)	804,000
	Depreciation separately disclosed	(418,000)
		1,186,000
d.	**Raw materials consumed**	
	Materials used	910,100
	Packing material	310,000
	Write-down to net realizable value	25,000
	Abnormal spillage	15,000
		1,260,100
e.	**Staff costs**	
	Labor	1,200,000
	Other staff costs	689,300
		1,889,300
f.	**Other operating expenses**	
	Distribution costs given	718,800
	Administrative costs given	929,100
	Operating costs given	587,100
	Staff costs shown in **calculation e**	(689,300)
	Depreciation separately shown	(205,000)
		1,340,700

CHAPTER 4

INVENTORIES (IAS 2)

4.1 PROBLEMS ADDRESSED

The accounting treatment of inventories under the historical cost system is prescribed. The primary issue is the calculation of the cost of inventory, which is to be recognized as an asset and carried forward until the related revenues are realized — the matching concept.

4.2 SCOPE OF THE STANDARD

The standard deals with all inventories that are assets:
- held for sale in the ordinary course of business, or
- in the process of production for sale, or
- in the form of materials or supplies to be consumed in the production process or
- in the rendering of services.

In the case of a service provider, inventories include the costs of the service for which the related revenue has not yet been recognized (e.g., work in progress of auditors, architects, and lawyers).

4.3 ACCOUNTING TREATMENT

4.3.1   Inventories should be measured at the lower of cost or net realizable value in accordance with the prudence concept.

4.3.2   **Cost of goods** comprise all costs of purchase, costs of conversion, and other costs incurred in bringing the inventories to their **present location and condition:**
- Purchase costs, such as the purchase price and import charges.
- Costs of conversion, being:
  - Direct labor.
  - Production overheads.
    - Variable overheads.
    - Fixed overheads allocated at normal production capacity.
- Other costs, such as design, borrowing costs, etc.

4.3.3   **Cost of services** comprise all costs directly engaged in providing the services, for example:
- Consumable goods.
- Labor and other staff costs.
- Attributable overheads.

4.3.4   The following **techniques** may be used to measure the cost of inventories:
- **Actual costs**
- **Standard cost**
  - Take into account normal levels of materials, labor and capacity.
  - Review regularly in order to approximate actual costs.
- **Retail method**
  - Apply when it is impractical to use actual costs.
  - Reduce sales value by gross margin to calculate 'cost.'
  - Average percentage is used for each homogeneous group of items.
  - Take into consideration marked down prices.

4.3.5   The actual cost of inventories may be assigned by using the following **cost formulas:**
- Specific identification.
- Weighted average cost.
- First-in, first-out (FIFO).
- Last-in, first-out (LIFO, Allowed alternative).

SIC–1 allows application of different cost formulas if the nature of groups of items differs from others.

4.3.6   **Net realizable value (NRV)** is the estimated selling price less the estimated costs of completion and costs necessary to make the sale. These estimates are based on the most reliable evidence at the time the estimates are made. The purpose for which the inventory is held should be taken into account at the time of the estimate. Inventories are usually written down to NRV based on the following principles:
- On an item-by-item basis.
- Similar items are normally grouped together.
- Each service is treated as a separate item.

4.3.7   The following items should be recognized as expenses in the income statement:
- Cost of inventories sold.
- Write-downs to NRV.
- Stock losses.
- Abnormal wastage.
- Non-allocated production overheads.

4.4   DISCLOSURE

The financial statements should disclose the following:
- Accounting policies, including the cost formulas used.
- Total carrying amount of inventories and amount per category.
- Amount of inventories carried at NRV.
- Amount of any reversal of any write-down.
- Circumstances/events that led to the reversal of a write-down.
- Inventories pledged as security for liabilities.
- Carrying amount of a write-down to NRV if significant in size, incidence, or nature.
- Costs of inventories recognized as an expense,

or

Operating costs, applicable to revenues, recognized as an expense, classified by their nature.
- When LIFO is used, show the difference between balance sheet amount and either:
  - lower of cost calculated on FIFO or weighted average and NRV, or
  - lower of current cost at year-end and NRV.

┌──────────────────────── CASE STUDY ────────────────────────┐

INVENTORIES

Arco Inc. is a manufacturing corporation in the food industry. The following matters relate to inventories of the corporation:

A.   In recent years the corporation utilized a standard costing system as an aid to management. The standard cost variances had been insignificant to date and were written off directly in the published annual financial statements. However, the following **two** problems were experienced during the year ending 31 March 20x3:

   •   Variances were of a far greater size as a result of a sharp increase in material and labor costs as well as a decrease in production.

   •   A large number of the units produced were unsold at year-end. This is partially attributable to the fact that the products of the company are "over-priced."

The management of the company intends, as in the past, to write off these variances directly as term costs, **and** to also write off a portion of the cost of surplus unsold inventories.

B.   Chocolate raw material inventories on hand at the end of the year represent eight months of usage. Inventory levels normally represent only two months' usage. The current replacement value of the inventories is less than the initial cost.

The above matters are treated as follows in the annual financial statements:

A.   Both proposed treatments are unacceptable.

   •   The write-offs of the large variances result in the standard values not approximating cost according to IAS 2 (see paragraph 4.3.4). Standard costs should be reviewed regularly and revised in the light of current conditions. The labor and material variances should be allocated to the standard cost of inventories. The production overhead variance resulting from idle capacity should be recognized as an expense in the current period.

   •   The term "over priced" is arbitrary and any write-down should be done only if the net realizable values of the products are lower than its cost (see paragraph 4.3.6).

B.   The abnormal portion of raw material on hand (representing six months of production) should be written down to a net realizable value. The other raw materials (representing two months of production) should only be written down to a net realizable value if the estimated cost of the **finished products** will be more than the net realizable value (see paragraph 4.3.6).

└──┘

CHAPTER 5

CASH FLOW STATEMENTS (IAS 7)

5.1 PROBLEMS ADDRESSED

Information about the historical changes in cash and cash equivalents of an enterprise is required in the form of a cash flow statement classifying cash flows during the reporting period from the **operating, investing**, and **financing activities**. Users require this information in order to form an opinion on:

- Changes in net assets.
- Financial structure of the enterprise.
- Solvency and liquidity of the enterprise.
- Ability of the enterprise to influence the amounts and timing of cash flows.
- Ability of the enterprise to generate cash.
- Present value of future cash flows of different enterprises (through models).

5.2 SCOPE OF THE STANDARD

All enterprises are required to present a cash flow statement that reports cash flows during the reporting period, classified as follows:

- **Operating activities:** Principal revenue-producing activities and other activities that do not include investing or financing activities.
- **Investing activities**: Acquisition and disposal of long-term assets and other investments not included in cash equivalents.
- **Financial activities:** Activities that change the size and composition of the equity capital and borrowings.

5.3 ACCOUNTING TREATMENT

5.3.1 Cash flows are inflows and outflows of both cash and cash equivalents.

5.3.2 **Cash** comprises:
- Cash on hand.
- Demand deposits (including bank overdrafts repayable on demand).

5.3.3 **Cash equivalents** are held for the purpose of meeting short-term cash commitments. They are short-term, highly liquid investments that readily convert to cash and that are subject to an insignificant risk of changes in value.

5.3.4 Cash flows from **operating activities** are reported directly or indirectly (the direct method is preferred by IAS 7):
- **Direct method**
  - Major classes of gross cash receipts and gross cash payments are disclosed.
  - A reconciliation between profit-before-tax and cash-generated-from-operations is given in a note to the cash flow statement.
- **Indirect method**
  - Profit/loss for the period is adjusted for:
  - Effects of non-cash transactions.
  - Deferrals or accruals.
  - Investing or financing cash flows.

5.3.5   Cash flows from **investing activities** are reported as follows:
- Major classes of **gross** cash receipts and **gross** cash payments are reported separately.
- The aggregate cash flows from acquisitions or disposals of subsidiaries and other business units are classified as investing.

5.3.6   Cash flows from **financing activities** are reported by separately listing major classes of **gross** cash receipts and **gross** cash payments.

5.3.7   The following cash flows are allowed to be reported on a **net** basis:
- Cash flows on behalf of customers.
- Items for which the turnover is quick, the amounts large, and maturities short (e.g. purchase and sale of investments).

5.3.8   The following cash flows of a financial institution may be reported on a **net** basis:
- Cash flows on behalf of customers.
- Items for which the turnover is quick, amounts large and maturities short.

5.3.9   The following aspects relate to the **presentation** of cash flow statements:
- The classification of interest and dividends received and paid is flexible. It should be treated consistently as either operating, investing, or financing activities.
- Cash flows from taxes on income are normally classified as operating.
- A forex transaction is recorded on the date of the cash flow.
- Foreign operations' cash flows are translated at exchange rates on dates of cash flows.
- An extraordinary item's cash flow should be classified according to the activity to which it belongs.
- When entities are equity- or cost-accounted, only actual cash flows from them are shown in the cash flow statement (e.g. dividends received).
- Cash flows from joint ventures are proportionately included in the cash flow statement.

5.4   DISCLOSURE

- Show in aggregate in respect of both the purchase or sale of a subsidiary or business unit:
  - Total purchase or disposal consideration.
  - Purchase or disposal consideration paid in cash and equivalents.
  - Amount of cash and equivalents in the entity acquired or disposed of.
  - Amount of assets and liabilities other than cash and equivalents in the entity acquired/disposed of.
- Cash and cash equivalents in the cash flow statement and a reconciliation with the equivalent items in the balance sheet.
- Details about non-cash investing and financing transactions (e.g. conversion of debt to equity).
- Amount of cash and equivalents that are not available for use by the group.
- Amount of undrawn borrowing facilities available for future operating activities and to settle capital commitments (indicating any restrictions).
- Aggregate amount of cash flows from each of the three activities related to interest in joint ventures.
- Amount of cash flows arising from each of the three activities regarding each reported business and geographical segment.
- Distinguish between the cash flows that represent an increase in operating capacity and those that represent the maintenance of it.

CASH FLOW STATEMENTS

The following are the abridged annual financial statements of Linco Inc.

INCOME STATEMENT FOR THE YEAR ENDING 30 SEPTEMBER 20x4

	$
Revenue	850,000
Cost of sales	(637,500)
Gross profit	212,500
Administrative expenses	(28,100)
Operating expenses	(73,600)
Profit from operations	110,800
Finance cost	(15,800)
Profit before tax	95,000
Income tax expense	(44,000)
Net profit for the period	51,000

STATEMENT OF CHANGES IN EQUITY FOR THE YEAR ENDING 30 SEPTEMBER 20x4

	Share capital $	Revaluation reserve $	Accumulated profit $	Total $
Balance — beginning of the	120,000		121,000	241,000
Revaluation of buildings		20,000		20,000
Net profit for the period			51,000	51,000
Dividends paid			(25,000)	(25,000)
Repayment of share capital	(20,000)			(20,000)
Balance — end of the year	100,000	20,000	147,000	267,000

BALANCE SHEET AT 30 SEPTEMBER 20x4

	20x4 $	20x3 $
ASSETS		
Non-current assets		
Property, plant and equipment		
Office buildings	250,000	220,000
Machinery	35,000	20,000
Motor vehicles	6,000	4,000
Long-term loans to directors	64,000	60,000
	355,000	304,000

CASE STUDY
CONTINUED

CASH FLOW STATEMENTS

Current assets

Inventories	82,000	42,000
Debtors	63,000	43,000
Prepaid expenses	21,000	16,000
Bank	-	6,000
	166,000	107,000
Total assets	**521,000**	**411,000**

EQUITY AND LIABILITIES

Capital and reserves

Share capital	100,000	120,000
Revaluation reserve	20,000	-
Accumulated profits	147,000	121,000
	267,000	241,000

Non-current liabilities

Long-term borrowings	99,000	125,000

Current liabilities

Creditors	72,000	35,000
Bank	43,000	-
Taxation due	40,000	10,000
	155,000	45,000
Total equity and liabilities	**521,000**	**411,000**

Additional information

1. The following depreciation charges are included in operating expenses:
    Machinery $25,000
    Motor vehicles $2,000
2. Fully depreciated machinery with an original cost price of $15,000, was sold for $5,000 during the year. The profit is included in operating expenses.
3. The financial manager mentions that the accountants allege the company is heading for a possible liquidity crisis. According to him the company struggled to meet its short-term obligations during the current year.

CASE STUDY
CONTINUED

CASH FLOW STATEMENTS

The cash flow statement would be presented as follows if the **direct method** was used for its preparation:

LINCO INC.
CASH FLOW STATEMENT FOR THE YEAR ENDING 30 SEPTEMBER 20x4

	$
Cash flows from operating activities	
Cash receipts from customers (**Calculation e**)	830,000
Cash payments to suppliers and employees (**Calculation f**)	(725,200)
Net cash generated by operations	104,800
Interest paid	(15,800)
Taxation paid (**Calculation d**)	(14,000)
Dividends paid	(25,000)
	50,000
Cash flows from investing activities	
Purchases of property, plant and equipment (**Calc. a, b, c**)	(54,000)
Proceeds on sale of machinery	5,000
Loans to directors	(4,000)
	(53,000)
Cash flows from financing activities	
Decrease in long-term loan (125 – 99)	(26,000)
Repayment of share capital	(20,000)
	(46,000)
Net decrease in bank balance for the period	(49,000)
Bank balance at beginning of the year	6,000
Overdraft at end of the year	**(43,000)**

COMMENTARY
1.   The total increase in creditors was used to partially finance the increase in working capital.
2.   The rest of the increase in working capital, the interest paid, taxation paid, and dividends paid, were financed by cash generated from operations.
3.   The remaining balance of cash generated by operating activities, as well as the proceeds on the sale of fixed assets, were used to finance the purchase of fixed assets.
4.   The overdrawn bank was used for the repayment of share capital and the redemption of the long-term loan.

CASE STUDY

CONTINUED

CASH FLOW STATEMENTS

CALCULATIONS

		$
a.	**Office buildings**	
	Balance at beginning of year	220,000
	Revaluation	20,000
	Purchases (balancing figure)	10,000
	Balance at end of the year	250,000
b.	**Machinery**	
	Balance at beginning of year	20,000
	Depreciation	(25,000)
	Purchases (balancing figure)	40,000
	Balance at end of the year	35,000
c.	**Vehicles**	
	Balance at beginning of year	4,000
	Depreciation	(2,000)
	Purchases (balancing figure)	4,000
	Balance at end of the year	6,000
d.	**Taxation**	
	Amount due at beginning of year	10,000
	Charge in income statement	44,000
	Paid in cash (balancing figure)	(14,000)
	Amount due at end of the year	40,000
e.	**Cash receipts from customers**	
	Sales	850,000
	Increase in debtors (63 – 43)	(20,000)
		830,000
f.	**Cash payments to suppliers and employees**	
	Cost of sales	637,500
	Administrative expenses	28,100
	Operating expenses	73,600
	Adjusted for non-cash flow items:	
	Depreciation	(27,000)
	Profit on sale of machinery	5,000
	Increase in inventories (82 – 42)	40,000
	Increase in creditors (72 – 35)	(37,000)
	Increase in prepaid expenses (21 – 16)	5,000
		725,200

CHAPTER 6

NET PROFIT OR LOSS FOR THE PERIOD, FUNDAMENTAL ERRORS, AND CHANGES IN ACCOUNTING POLICIES (IAS 8)

6.1 PROBLEMS ADDRESSED

The standard describes the classification, accounting treatment, and disclosure of selected items in the income statement to ensure that all enterprises treat them consistently.

6.2 SCOPE OF THE STANDARD

This standard should be applied in presenting profit or loss from ordinary activities, extraordinary items, as well as in the accounting for changes in accounting estimates, fundamental errors, and changes in accounting policies.

6.3 ACCOUNTING TREATMENT

6.3.1 **Results from ordinary activities** are those activities undertaken by an enterprise as part of its business and such related activities in which the enterprise engages. These results are included in profit before tax.

Income and expense items within profit or loss from ordinary activities that are of such size, nature or incidence that their disclosure is relevant to explain the performance of the enterprise for the period, should be disclosed separately (e.g., inventory write-downs, costs of restructuring, discontinuing operations, etc.).

6.3.2 **Extraordinary items** are income or expenses that arise from events or transactions that are clearly distinct from the ordinary activities of the enterprise and therefore are not expected to recur frequently (e.g., expropriations and natural disasters).

Extraordinary items are treated as a single line item on the face of the income statement, separate from profit or loss from ordinary activities.

6.3.3 **Changes in accounting estimates** relate to uncertainties inherent in business activities resulting in many items that cannot be measured with precision but can only be estimated. When difficult to distinguish between a change in accounting policy or a change in estimate, the latter is chosen.

The effect of such a change is included in the net profit or loss for the current period, or the current and future periods if the change affects both.

6.3.4 **Fundamental errors** are errors discovered in the current period that are of such significance that financial statements of previous period(s) can no longer be considered reliable at date of issue.

Benchmark treatment:
- Adjust opening balance of accumulated profits.
- Income statement comparatives are restated.
- Other reported comparatives are restated.

Allowed alternative:
- The amount of the correction is included net profit or loss for the current period.
- Comparatives are not restated.
- Pro-forma comparatives are furnished.

6.3.5   **Change in accounting policies:** Accounting policies are the specific principles, bases, conventions, rules, and practices adopted by an enterprise in preparing and presenting financial statements. They are applied consistently from period to period. A **change** in accounting policy is allowable under one of the following conditions only:
- Required by statute.
- Required by an accounting standard-setting body (i.e., adoption of an IAS).
- The change will result in a more appropriate presentation.

Benchmark treatment:
- Refer to any transitional provisions for the adoption of an IAS.
- Apply retrospectively:
  - Adjust opening accumulated profits.
  - Restate comparatives.
- Apply prospectively if impracticable to restate prior period(s).

Allowed alternative:
- The amount of retrospective application of the change in policy is included in net profit or loss for the current period.
- Comparatives are not restated.
- Pro-forma comparatives are furnished.
- Prospective application is allowed if retrospective application is impracticable.

6.4   DISCLOSURE

6.4.1   **Separately disclosable items** within profit/loss from ordinary activities
- Nature.
- Amount before and after tax.

6.4.2   **Extraordinary items**
- Nature.
- Amount.
- Tax effect.
- Minority interest.

6.4.3   **Change in accounting estimates**
- Nature.
- Amount before and after tax.

6.4.4   **Fundamental errors**
- Nature.
- Amount of correction in current and previous periods.
- Tax effect.
- Minority interest.
- Fact that comparatives are restated.
- Reason if comparatives are not restated.

6.4.5 Change in accounting policies
- Reason(s) for change.
- Amount adjusted in current and previous periods.
- Tax effect.
- Minority interest.
- Fact that comparatives are restated.
- Reason for comparatives not being restated.

CASE STUDY

NET PROFIT OR LOSS FOR THE PERIOD, FUNDAMENTAL ERRORS, AND CHANGES IN ACCOUNTING POLICIES

Unicurio Inc. is a manufacturer of curios that are sold at international airports. The following unusual transactions and events occurred during the year under review:

1. A $1.9 million adjustment was made to the provision for depreciation on the review of the expected life and use of the plant.

2. Bonuses of $12 million, compared to $2.3 million of the previous year, had been paid to employees. The financial manager explains that a new incentive scheme was adopted whereby all employees shared in increased sales.

3. There was a $1.25 million profit on the expropriation by government of land that was shown at fair value in the financial statements.

4. During the year the corporation was responsible for the formation of the ECA Foundation, which donates funds to welfare organizations. This foundation forms part of the corporation's social investment program. The company contributed $7 million to the fund.

Each of the transactions and events mentioned above would be **treated** as follows **in the income statement** for the current year:

1. This is a change in accounting estimate (see paragraph 6.3.3), which should be included in profit or loss from ordinary activities. The nature and amount of the change in accounting estimate that has a material effect in the current period should be disclosed (normally in a note).

2. Due to its nature and size, this is a separately disclosable item within profit or loss from ordinary activities (see paragraph 6.3.1). The nature and amount of the item should be disclosed separately.

3. This is an extraordinary item (see paragraph 6.3.2), which is clearly distinct from the ordinary activities. The nature and amount of the item should be disclosed separately and not as part of profit or loss from ordinary activities.

4. The social upliftment program is part of ordinary activities. The amount could be shown separately, if it were abnormal in size compared to previous years. Otherwise, it should be included as a non-disclosable item in profit or loss from ordinary activities.

CHAPTER 7

EVENTS AFTER
THE BALANCE SHEET DATE (IAS 10)

7.1 PROBLEMS ADDRESSED

The standard prescribes the appropriate accounting treatment for events that occur subsequent to the balance sheet date but before the date that the financial statements are approved for issue. These events may indicate the need for adjustments to the amounts recognized in the financial statements or require disclosure.

7.2 SCOPE OF THE STANDARD

The standard should be applied in the accounting and disclosure of all post-balance sheet events, both favorable and unfavorable, that occur before the date on which the financial statements are authorized for issue.

7.3 ACCOUNTING TREATMENT

7.3.1 Two types of events can be distinguished:
- Adjusting events providing additional evidence of conditions existing **at** the balance sheet date (the origin of the event is in the current reporting period).
- Non-adjusting events indicative of conditions arising **after** the balance sheet date.

7.3.2 The process of **authorization** for issue of financial statements will depend on the form of the enterprise and its management structure. The date of authorization for issue would normally be the date on which the financial statements are authorized for issue outside the enterprise.

7.3.3 Amounts recognized in the financial statements of an enterprise are **adjusted** for events occurring after the balance sheet date that provide additional information about conditions existing at the balance sheet date, and therefore allow these amounts to be estimated more accurately (e.g., adjustments may be required for a loss recognized on a trade debtor that is confirmed by the bankruptcy of a customer after the balance sheet date).

7.3.4 If events occur after the balance sheet date that do not affect the condition of assets and liabilities at the balance sheet date, **no adjustment** is required. However, disclosure should be made of such events if they are of such importance that non-disclosure would affect decisions made by users of the financial statements (e.g., if an earthquake destroys a major portion of the manufacturing plant of the enterprise after the balance sheet date).

7.3.5 Dividends stated should be in respect of the period covered by the financial statements; those that are proposed or declared after the balance sheet date but before approval of the financial statements should not be recognized as a liability at the balance sheet date. An enterprise may give the required disclosure of such dividends either on the face of the balance sheet as a separate component of equity or in the notes to the financial statements.

7.3.6   An enterprise should not prepare financial statements on a going concern basis if management determines after the balance sheet date either that it intends to liquidate the enterprise or to cease trading, or that it has no realistic alternative but to do the aforementioned.

7.4   DISCLOSURE

7.4.1   Date of authorization for issue

- Date when financial statements were authorized for issue.
- Who gave the authorization.
- If any party has the power to amend the financial statements after issuance, this fact should be stated.

7.4.2   Non-adjusting events

For non-adjusting events that would affect the ability of the users to make proper evaluations and decisions, the following should be disclosed:

- Nature of the event.
- Estimate of the financial effect.
- A statement if such an estimate cannot be made.

7.4.3   Updating disclosures on conditions at balance sheet date

Update disclosures that relate to conditions that existed at the balance sheet date, in light of any new information about those conditions that is received after the balance sheet date.

CASE STUDY

Events After the Balance Sheet Date

A corporation with a balance sheet date of 31 December has a foreign long-term liability that is not covered by a foreign exchange contract. The foreign currency amount was converted at the closing rate on 31 December 20x4 and is shown in the accounting records at the local currency, LC2.0 million.

The local currency dropped significantly against the US dollar on 27 February 20x5. On this date, management decided to hedge further exposure by taking out a foreign currency forward exchange contract, which limited the eventual liability to LC6.0 million. If this situation were to apply at the balance sheet date, it would result in the corporation's liabilities exceeding the fair value of its assets.

The situation under discussion falls within the definition of **post-balance sheet events** and specifically those events that refer to conditions arising after the balance sheet date.

The loss of LC4.0 million that arises in 20x5 must be recognized in the 20x5 income statement. No provision in respect of the loss may be made in the financial statements for the year ending 31 December 20x4.

However, consideration should be given to whether it would be appropriate to apply the **going concern** concept in the preparation of the financial statements. The date and frequency of repayment of the liability will have to be considered.

The following information should be **disclosed in a note** to the financial statements for the year ending 31 December 20x4:
- The nature of the events.
- An estimate of the financial effect, in this case LC4.0 million.

Chapter 8

Construction Contracts (IAS 11)

PROBLEMS ADDRESSED

The standard deals with the accounting treatment of construction contract revenue and costs, with a focus on:
- Proper matching of contract revenue and related costs.
- The allocation of contract revenue and costs to the accounting periods in which construction work is performed.

SCOPE OF THE STANDARD

Those construction contracts of which the dates of contracting and of completion typically fall in different accounting periods. They include contracts for:
- Rendering of services.
- Destruction or restoration of assets and the restoration of the environment.

ACCOUNTING TREATMENT

8.3.1 Two types of contracts are distinguished, namely:
- **Fixed price contracts** usually a fixed contract price subject to cost escalation clauses.
- **Cost plus contracts** the contract costs plus a percentage of these costs or a fixed fee.

8.3.2 The principles of the IAS are normally applied separately to each contract, which may be specifically negotiated for the construction of:
- an asset, (e.g., a bridge), or
- a combination of assets that are closely interrelated or interdependent in terms of their **design**, **technology** and **function/use** (e.g., specialized production plants).

A group of contracts should be treated as a **single** construction contract if it was negotiated as a single package.

8.3.3 The following contracts should be treated as **separate** construction contracts:
- A contract for a number of assets if separate proposals have been submitted for each asset.
- An additional asset constructed at the option of the customer that was not part of the original contract.

8.3.4 **Contract revenue** comprise:
- The initial agreed contract amount.
- Variations, claims, and incentive payments to the extent that:
  - it is probable that they will realize, and
  - they are capable of being reliably measured.

31

8.3.5   **Contract costs** comprise:
- Direct contract costs (e.g., materials).
- General contract costs (e.g., insurance).
- Costs specifically chargeable to the customer in terms of the contract (e.g., administrative costs).

8.3.6   If the **outcome** of a construction contract can be estimated reliably, revenue and costs (profit) should be recognized based on the stage of completion (percentage of completion method). Methods to determine the stage of completion include:
- Portion of costs incurred in relation to estimated total costs.
- Surveys of work performed.
- Physical stage of completion.

8.3.7   Contract revenue is recognized based on the work performed during the accounting period. The related contract costs of the work performed is recognized accordingly and **matched** with the income in order to determine the contract profit for the period.

8.3.8   If the outcome of a contract cannot be reliably estimated (e.g., at the early stages of a contract):
- Recognize revenue to the extent that it is probable to recover contract costs.
- Recognize contract costs incurred.

8.3.9   Any expected excess of **total** contract costs over **total** contract revenue is recognized as an expense immediately.

8.4   DISCLOSURE

Accounting policies
- Methods used for revenue recognition.
- Methods used for stage of completion.

Income statement
- Amount of contract revenue recognized.

Balance sheet and notes
- Amount of advances received.
- Amount of retention monies.
- Contracts in progress being costs-to-date-plus-profits or costs-to-date-less-losses.
- Gross amount due from customers (assets).
- Gross amount due to customers (liabilities).
- Contingent assets and contingent liabilities (e.g., claims).

CASE STUDY

CONSTRUCTION CONTRACTS

Omega Inc. started a four-year contract to build a dam. Activities commenced on 1 February 20x3. The total contract price amounted to $12,000,000, and it was estimated that the work would be completed at a total cost of $9,500,000. In the construction agreement the customer agreed to accept increases in wage tariffs additional to the contract price.

The following information refers to contract activities for the financial year ending 31 December 20x3:

1. Costs for the year:

		$
•	Material	1,400,000
•	Labor	800,000
•	Operating overheads	150,000
•	Subcontractors	180,000

2. Current estimate of total contract costs indicates as follows:
   - Materials to be $180,000 higher than expected.
   - Total labor costs to be $300,000 higher than expected. Of this amount, only $240,000 would be brought about by increased wage tariffs. The other amount would be due to inefficiencies.
   - A savings of $30,000 is expected on operating overheads.

3. During the current financial year the customer requested a variation to the original contract and it was agreed that the contract price would be increased by $900,000. The total estimated cost of this extra work is $750,000.

4. By the end of 20x3, certificates issued by quantity surveyors indicated a 25% stage of completion.

CONTRACT PROFIT RECOGNIZED FOR THE YEAR ENDING 31 DECEMBER 20x3:

	Option 1 $'000	Option 2 $'000
Contract revenue (Calculation d)	3,107	3,285
Contract costs to date (Calculation a)	(2,530)	(2,530)
	577	755

CALCULATIONS	$'000
a. **Contract costs**	
• Materials	1,400
• Labor	800
• Operating overheads	150
• Subcontractors	180
	2,530

────── CASE STUDY ──────

CONTINUED

CONSTRUCTION CONTRACTS

b. **Revised estimated total costs until end of contract**

• Original estimate	9,500
• Materials	180
• Labor	300
• Operating overheads	(30)
• Variation	750
	10,700

c. **Amended contract price**

• Original amount	12,000
• Labor (wage increases added to contract price)	240
• Variation	900
	13,140

d. **Contract revenue**

	Option 1	Option 2
Based on contract costs **in proportion to** estimated total contract costs:		
2,530 ÷ 10,700 x 13,140 (rounded off)	3,107	
Based on work certified: 25% x 13,140		3,285

CHAPTER 9

INCOME TAXES (IAS 12)

<table>
<tr><td>9.1</td><td>PROBLEMS ADDRESSED</td></tr>
</table>

The IAS addresses the principle of how to account for the current and future tax consequences of:

- The future recovery (settlement) of the carrying amount of assets (liabilities) in the balance sheet.
- Transactions and other events of the current period that are recognized in an enterprise's financial statements.

<table>
<tr><td>9.2</td><td>SCOPE OF THE STANDARD</td></tr>
</table>

This standard deals with all income taxes **including** domestic, foreign, and withholding taxes as well as income tax consequences of dividend payments.

<table>
<tr><td>9.3</td><td>ACCOUNTING TREATMENT</td></tr>
</table>

9.3.1 **Current tax** is the amount of income taxes payable or recoverable in respect of the current period.

9.3.2 **Deferred tax** is the amount of income taxes payable or recoverable in **future periods** in respect of:
- Temporary differences.
- Carry forward of unused tax losses.
- Carry forward of unused tax credits.

9.3.3 **Temporary differences** are differences between the tax base of an item and its carrying amount, being:
- **Taxable temporary differences** resulting in taxable amounts in future periods.
  or
- **Deductible temporary differences** resulting in amounts that are deductible from income taxes that become payable in future periods.

9.3.4 The **tax base** of an item is the amount attributed to that item for tax purposes by tax authorities.

9.3.5 **Current tax balances** should be recognized as follows:
- Raise a liability (asset) for unpaid (overpaid) current taxes.
- Benefit of a tax loss carried back should be recognized as an asset.

9.3.6 A **deferred tax liability** is recognized for all taxable temporary differences, except when it arises from:
- goodwill for which amortization is not deductible for tax purposes, or
- the initial recognition of an asset or liability in a transaction which:
  - is not a business combination, **and**
  - at the time of the transaction affects neither accounting nor taxable profit.

9.3.7 A **deferred tax asset** is recognized for deductible temporary differences to the extent that it is **probably** recoverable from future taxable profits. A deferred tax asset is not recognized when it arises from:
- the initial recognition of an asset or liability in a transaction which:
  - is not a business combination, **and**
  - at the time of the transaction affects neither accounting nor taxable profit.

9.3.8 A deferred tax asset is recognized for the carry forward of **unused tax losses/credits** to the extent that it is **probably** recoverable in the future.

9.3.9 Temporary differences arise when the carrying amount of investments in **subsidiaries, branches, associates, and joint ventures** becomes different from the tax base thereof.

9.3.10 The following principles apply to the **measurement** of current and deferred tax balances:
- These liabilities (assets) are to be measured at amounts to be paid (recovered) using tax rates (and tax laws) that have been substantively enacted by the reporting date.
- Deferred tax balances should reflect the tax consequences regarding how the asset is to be recovered or liability settled.
- Current and deferred tax assets and liabilities are measured at the tax rate applicable to undistributed profits.
- The income tax consequences of dividends are recognized when a liability to pay the dividend is recognized.
- Discounting is prohibited.
- Impairment tests should be performed on deferred tax assets at each balance sheet date.

9.3.11 Current and deferred tax should be recognized as income/expense and **included in the income statement**, except tax arising from:
- A transaction or event that is recognized directly in equity.
- A business combination that is an acquisition.

9.4 PRESENTATION & DISCLOSURE

9.4.1 PRESENTATION

Taxation balances should be presented as follows:
- Tax balances are shown separately from other assets and liabilities in the balance sheet.
- Deferred tax balances are distinguished from current tax balances.
- Deferred tax balances are **non**-current.
- Show taxation expense (income) for ordinary activities on the face of the income statement.
- May **offset** current tax balances when:
  - Legal enforceable right to offset.
  - Intention to settle on net basis.
- May **offset** deferred tax balances when:
  - Legal enforceable right to offset.
  - Debits and credits relate to same tax authority:
    - for the same taxable entity, or
    - different taxable entities that intend to settle on net basis.

9.4.2   DISCLOSURE

Accounting policy

- Method used for deferred tax.

Income statement and notes

- Major components of tax expense (income) shown separately, including:
  - Current tax expense (income).
  - Deferred tax expense (income).
  - Deferred tax arising from the write-down (or reversal of a previous write-down) of a deferred tax asset.
  - Tax amount relating to changes in accounting policies and fundamental errors treated in accordance with IAS 8 allowed alternative.
- Tax relating to extraordinary items.
- Reconciliation between tax amount and accounting profit/loss in monetary terms, or a numerical reconciliation of the rate.
- Explanation of changes in applicable tax rate(s) compared to previous period(s).
- For each type of temporary difference, and in respect of each type of unused tax losses and credits, the amounts of the deferred tax recognized in the income statement.

Balance sheet and notes

- Aggregate amount of **current** and **deferred** tax charged or credited to equity.
- Amount (and expiration date) of deductible temporary differences, unused tax losses, and unused tax credits for which no deferred tax asset is recognized.
- Aggregate amount of temporary differences associated with investments in subsidiaries, branches, associates, and joint ventures for which deferred tax liabilities have not been recognized.
- For each type of temporary difference, and in respect of each type of unused tax losses and credits, the amount of the deferred tax assets and liabilities recognized in the balance sheet.
- Amount of a deferred tax asset and nature of the evidence supporting its recognition, when:
  - The utilization of the deferred tax asset is dependent on future taxable profits.
  - The enterprise has suffered a loss in either the current or preceding period.
- Amount of income tax consequences of dividends to shareholders that were proposed or declared before the balance sheet date, but are not recognized as a liability in the financial statements.
- The nature of the potential income tax consequences that would result from the payment of dividends to the enterprises' shareholders, i.e., the important features of the income tax systems and the factors that will effect the amount of the potential tax consequences of dividends.

CASE STUDY

INCOME TAXES

Difir Inc. owns the following property, plant, and equipment at 31 December 20x4:

	Cost $'000	Accumulated depreciation $'000	Carrying amount $'000	Tax base $'000
Machinery	900	180	720	450
Land	500	–	500	n/a
Buildings	1,500	300	1,200	n/a

Additional information

- Machinery is depreciated on the straight-line basis over 5 years. It was acquired on 1 January 20x4.
- Land is not depreciated.
- Buildings comprising the office space of the corporation are depreciated on the straight-line basis over 25 years.
- No depreciation is allowed on land and office buildings for tax purposes. For machinery, a depreciation allowance is granted over a period of three years in the ratio of 50/30/20 (percent) of cost consecutively.
- The accounting profit before tax amounted to $300,000 for the 20x5 financial year and $400,000 for 20x6. These figures include non-taxable revenue at the amount of $80,000 in 20x5 and $100,000 in 20x6.
- Difir Inc. had a tax loss on 31 December 20x4 of $250,000. The tax rate for 20x4 was 35%, and for 20x5 and 20x6 it was 30%.

The movements on the deferred tax balance for 20x5 and 20x6 will be reflected as follows in the accounting records of the enterprise:

Deferred tax liability	**$'000 Dr/(Cr)**
1 Jan. 20x5 Balance	
• Machinery **(Calculation a)**	(94.5)
• Assessed loss (250 x 35%)	87.5
	(7.0)
Rate change (7 x 5/35)	1.0
Temporary differences: –Machinery **(Calculation a)**	(27.0)
–Loss utilized **(Calculation b, 190 x 30%)**	(57.0)
31 Dec. 20x5 Balance	(90.0)
Temporary difference: –Machinery **(Calculation a)**	–
31 Dec. 20x6 Loss utilized **(Calculation b, 60 x 30%)**	(18.0)
31 Dec. 20x6 Balance	(108.0)

CASE STUDY

CONTINUED

INCOME TAXES

CALCULATIONS

a.   Machinery

	Carrying amount $'000	Tax base $'000	Temporary difference $'000	Deferred tax $'000
1 Jan. 20x4 Purchase	900	900		
Depreciation	(180)	(450)	270	94.5
31 Dec. 20x4	720	450	270	94.5
Rate change (5/35 x 94.5)				(13.5)
Depreciation	(180)	(270)	90	27.0
31 Dec. 20x5	540	180	360	108.0
Depreciation	(180)	(180)	–	–
31 Dec. 20x6	360	–	360	108.0

b.   Income tax expense

	20x6 $'000	20x5 $'000
Accounting profit before tax	400	300
Tax effect of items not deductible/taxable for tax purposes:		
• Non-taxable revenue	(100)	(80)
• Depreciation on buildings (1500/25)	60	60
	360	280
Temporary differences:	–	(90)
• Depreciation: accounting	180	180
• Depreciation: tax	(180)	(270)
	360	190
Assessed loss brought forward	(60)	(250)
Taxable profit/(tax loss)	300	(60)
Tax payable/(benefit) @ 30%	90	(18)

CHAPTER 10

SEGMENT REPORTING (IAS 14)

Principles are established for reporting information by segment; that is, information about the different types of products and services of an enterprise and the different geographical areas in which it operates. This is relevant to help users:

- understand the enterprise's past performance,
- assess the enterprise's risks and returns, and
- make more informed judgements.

This standard applies to all enterprises whose equity or debt securities are traded in a public securities market or those who are in the process of issuing such instruments. A parent enterprise presents segment information only on the basis of consolidated financial statements. Segment information is presented for both **business** and **geographical** segments.

- **Business segment**: A distinguishable component of an enterprise engaged in providing products or services that are subject to risks and returns that are different from those of other business segments (e.g., industrial, agricultural, and financial segments).
- **Geographical segment**: A distinguishable component of an enterprise engaged in providing products or services in a particular economic environment that is subject to risks and returns that are different from those components operating in other economic environments. Geographical segments could be based either on the location of an enterprise's:
  - operations, **or**
  - markets and customers.

10.3.1 An enterprise's organizational and managerial structure and its internal financial reporting system is the basis for identifying its segments — often called the "management approach." This approach normally provides the best evidence of the enterprise's **predominant source of risks and returns** for the purpose of segmental reporting. This would then become the **primary segment** reporting format and the secondary source of risks and returns becomes its **secondary segment** reporting format. If, however, internal segments develops that relate to neither related products and services nor geographical areas (e.g., reporting is organized solely by the legal form of the entities in a group), then the next level of internal segmentation (that reports along product and service or geographical lines) should be used.

10.3.2 A business or geographical segment is a **reportable segment** if both of the following apply:
- Majority (greater than 50%) of its sales is earned externally.
- Its revenue from sales, segment result, or assets is greater than or equal to 10% of the appropriate total amount of all segments.

If the total revenue from external customers for all reportable segments combined is less than 75% of the total enterprise revenue, additional reportable segments should be identified until the 75% level is reached.

10.3.3 Small segments may be combined as one if they share a substantial number of factors that define a business or geographical segment, **or** they may be combined with a similar significant reportable segment. If they are not separately reported or combined, they are included as an unallocated reconciling item.

10.3.4 A segment that is not judged to be a reportable segment in the current period (in terms of the conditions in 10.3.2) should continue to be reportable if judged to be of significance for decision making purposes (e.g., future market strategy).

10.3.5 **Segment result** is a measure of operating profit before corporate head office expenses, interest income or expense (except for financial segments), income taxes, extraordinary items, investment gains and losses (again, except for financial segments), and minority interest deduction. It includes proportionately consolidated revenue and expenses from joint ventures and all equity- accounted profits/losses.

10.3.6 **Segment assets and liabilities** are identified as follows:
- It includes all operating assets and liabilities that are used by or result from a segment's operating activities and that either are directly attributable to the segment or can be allocated to the segment on a reasonable basis.
- Symmetry is required for the inclusion of items in the segment result and in segment assets or liabilities. If, for example, the segment result reflects depreciation expense, the depreciable asset must be included in segment assets. Similarly, if the segment result includes interest expense, the interest-bearing liabilities should be included in segment liabilities.
- Income tax assets/liabilities are excluded.
- Assets that are jointly used by two or more segments should be allocated to segments only if their related revenues and expenses also are allocated to those segments.

10.3.7 Segment information should conform to the **accounting policies** adopted for preparing and presenting the consolidated financial statements.

10.4   DISCLOSURE

10.4.1 **Primary segment information**
For **each** segment, disclose:
- Segment revenue distinguishing between sales to external customers and revenue from other segments.
- Segment result.
- Carrying amount of segment assets.
- Segment liabilities.
- Cost of property, plant, and equipment, and intangible assets acquired.
- Depreciation and amortization expense.
- Other non-cash expenses.
- Share of the net profit or loss of an investment accounted for under the equity method.
- A reconciliation between the information of reportable segments and the consolidated financial statements in terms of segment revenue, result, assets, and liabilities.

10.4.2 Secondary segment information

For **each** segment, disclose:

- Revenue from external customers.
- Carrying amount of segment assets.
- Cost of property, plant, and equipment, and intangible assets acquired.

10.4.3 Other required disclosures:

- Revenue of any segment whereby the external revenue of the segment is greater than or equal to 10% of enterprise revenue but that is not a reportable segment (because a majority of its revenue is from internal transfers).
- Basis of pricing intersegment transfers.
- Changes in segment accounting policies.
- Types of products and services in each business segment.
- Composition of each geographical segment.

CASE STUDY

SEGMENT REPORTING

Hollier Inc. is a diversified entity that operates in five business segments and four geographical segments. The following financial information relates to the year ending 30 June 20x5.

Business segment data (in $'000)

	Beer	Beverages	Hotels	Retail	Packaging	Total
Total revenue from sales	2,249	1,244	4,894	3,815	7,552	19,754
• To external customers	809	543	4,029	3,021	5,211	13,613
• To other segments	1,440	701	865	794	2,341	6,141
Segment result	631	(131)	714	(401)	1,510	2,323
Assets	4,977	3,475	5,253	1,072	8,258	23,035

Geographical segment data (in $'000)

	Finland	France	UK	Australia	Total
Total revenue from sales	7,111	1,371	3,451	7,821	19,754
• To external customers	6,841	1,000	2,164	3,608	13,613
• To other segments	270	371	1,287	4,213	6,141
Segment result	1,536	(478)	494	771	2,323
Assets	9,231	5,001	3,667	5,136	23,035

The **first** step in identifying the reportable business and geographical segments of the enterprise is to identify those who earn the majority of its revenue from sales to external customers.

Segments	% sales external	Qualify?
Business		
• Beer	809/2,249 = 36%	No
• Beverages	543/1,244 = 44%	No
• Hotels	4,029/4,894 = 82%	Yes
• Retail	3,021/3,815 = 79%	Yes
• Packaging	5,211/7,552 = 69%	Yes
Geographical		
• Finland	6,841/7,111 = 96%	Yes
• France	1,000/1,371 = 73%	Yes
• UK	2,164/3,451 = 63%	Yes
• Australia	3,608/7,821 = 46%	No

CASE STUDY
CONTINUED

Segment Reporting

The **second** step would be to ensure that the 10% thresholds for revenue from either sales, segment result, or assets are being met by those segments that qualified under step one. The thresholds are calculated as follows.

	$
• Sales (10% x 19,754)	1,976
• Segment result	
▪ Business: [10% of the greater of (631 + 714 + 1,510) or (131 + 401)]	286
▪ Geographical: [10% of the greater of (1,536 + 494 + 771) or 478]	280
• Assets (10% x 23,035)	2,304

Segments	Thresholds that qualified	Reportable?
Business		
• Hotels	Sales, Result, Assets	Yes
• Retail	Sales, Result	Yes
• Packaging	Sales, Result, Assets	Yes
Geographical		
• Finland	Sales, Result, Assets	Yes
• France	Result, Assets	Yes
• UK	Sales, Result, Assets	Yes

The **third** step would be to check if total external revenue attributable to reportable segments constitutes at least 75% of the total consolidated/enterprise revenue of $13,613,000.
- Reportable business segments' external revenue is $12,261,000 (4,029 + 3,021 + 5,211) which is 90% of total sales revenue.
- Reportable geographical segments' external revenue is $10,005,000 (6,841 + 1,000 + 2,164), which is 73.5% of total sales revenue and less than 75%.

In terms of IAS 14 (par. 37), additional geographical segments should now be identified as reportable even if they do not meet the 10% thresholds in step two. This would mean that Australia would, under this requirement, also qualify to be a reportable geographical segment (see paragraph 10.3.2).

The reportable segments would be as follows:
- **Business**: Hotels, Retail, and Packaging.
- **Geographical**: Finland, France, UK, and Australia.

CHAPTER 11

INFORMATION REFLECTING THE EFFECTS OF CHANGING PRICES (IAS 15)

11.1 PROBLEMS ADDRESSED

Financial statements are normally prepared on the historical cost basis without reflecting the effects of changing prices. The information required by IAS 15 is designed to make users of an enterprise's financial statements aware of the effects of changing prices on the results of operations. Compliance with IAS 15 is encouraged but not compulsory; non-compliance would therefore not result in a qualified audit report.

11.2 SCOPE OF THE STANDARD

The standard is applicable to entities that are significant in the economic environment in which they operate.

11.3 ACCOUNTING TREATMENT

11.3.1 Financial information on changing prices is prepared in various ways, namely:
- In terms of general purchasing power.
- Current cost instead of historical cost.
- Hybrid method.

11.3.2 Under the **general purchasing power approach**, income is recognized after the general purchasing power of the shareholders' equity has been maintained (the concept of financial capital maintenance in the Framework; see paragraph 2.3.10):
- Some or all items in the financial statements are restated for changes in the general price level, using an appropriate index.
- Income normally reflects the effects of general price level changes on depreciation, cost of sales, and net monetary items.

11.3.3 Under the **current cost approach,** the replacement cost of an asset is used as the primary measurement basis. Income is recognized after the operating capacity has been maintained (the concept of physical capital maintenance of the Framework; see paragraph 2.3.10):
- Current cost methods generally require recognition of the effects of changes in prices on depreciation, and the cost of sales.
- These methods usually also require the application of some form of adjustments that have in common a general recognition of the interaction between changing prices and the financing of an enterprise.

11.3.4 Financial information is sometimes provided using the various methods described above, either in primary or supplementary financial statements. However, there is not yet international consensus on the subject.

11.4   DISCLOSURE

The following information should be provided on a **supplementary** basis unless such information forms part of the primary financial statements:

- Methods adopted.
- Nature of indices used.
- Adjustment to or adjusted amount of depreciation of property, plant, and equipment.
- Adjustment to or the adjusted amount of cost of sales.
- Adjustments relating to monetary items, the effect of borrowing, or equity interests when such adjustments have been taken into account in determining income.
- Overall effect on results of the latter three adjustments described above, as well as any other items reflecting the effects of changing prices that are reported.
- When a current cost method is adopted, the current cost of property, plant, and equipment as well as inventories should be disclosed.

CASE STUDY

INFORMATION REFLECTING THE
EFFECTS OF CHANGING PRICES

The managing director of a manufacturing corporation questions the benefits of preparing and presenting information in the financial statements that would reflect the effects of changing prices on the operating results and financial position of the corporation. He asks the following questions:

- What are the limitations of historical cost accounting?
- What are the main items to be adjusted in the financial statements in order to reflect the effects of changing prices, and what is the purpose of such adjustments?

Limitations of historical cost accounting

Financial statements prepared on the historical cost basis do not necessarily lead to a true and fair presentation of an entity's performance or future potential if capital is not being maintained. Furthermore, actual assessment of performance through ratios such as return on capital are meaningless if profits are overstated, capital undervalued, and assets are valued under a mixture of conventions.

Limitations of historical cost accounting include:

- Depreciation charged on historically costed assets is only an arbitrary amount based on out-of-date values and estimated useful economic lives.
- Depreciation charges do not take into account actual replacement cost of assets at current prices.
- Profit will not reflect the actual 'costs' of trading, which include the replacement of assets at some point in time.
- By not accounting for inflation, there is no assurance that the entity is maintaining its capital base.
- Overstating profits by undercharging depreciation based on historical cost, and charging cost of sales at historical cost of inventories (and not current cost) can lead to the depletion of an entity's capital through high tax charges and distributions.
- While historical cost accounting provides a consistent basis for entities to prepare accounts, inflation affects different products and markets, and hence entities, to different degrees.
- Historical cost accounting makes it difficult for shareholders and analysts to assess the real performance and ability of management because changes to current market conditions are not accounted for in the historical valuation basis.
- The true valuation of entities is difficult to assess under historical cost rules.
- Interpretation of accounts over a period of time is difficult because each year relates to different purchasing powers.
- Key ratios (such as return on total assets) are inflated under historical rules because profit is overstated (as outlined above) and total assets are understated since assets are undervalued compared to current costs. Therefore, entities investing in new assets, (which lead to increased efficiencies and profits), will be penalized under such ratio analysis due to higher total assets, effectively stated at current costs.

Main adjustments

- **Costs of sales**: The objective is to calculate the current cost of goods sold during the period at the actual or weighted date that the sales occurred. The net profit is reduced by this adjustment.
- **Depreciation**: The core of this adjustment is that the depreciable amount of property, plant, and equipment be adjusted to current value. The depreciation charge for the period is then based on this value. The net profit is reduced by this adjustment.

CASE STUDY

CONTINUED

INFORMATION REFLECTING THE
EFFECTS OF CHANGING PRICES

- **Gearing adjustment**: This is an adjustment that is based on the manner in which the non-monetary assets are being financed within an entity:
  - External resources could be used to partially finance the cost of replacement of non-monetary assets (this would occur when monetary liabilities exceed monetary assets and no loss in purchasing power is suffered by the owners). The **net** monetary liability position even enables the entity to finance a portion of non-monetary assets, which neutralize a portion of the costs of replacement of inventories as well as property, plant, and equipment. The net profit will be increased by such an adjustment.
  - If monetary assets exceed monetary liabilities, a situation exists where all of the costs of replacement of inventory and property, plant, and equipment as well as the **net** portion of monetary assets are financed by equity. This would have a negative effect on net profit for the period because of the loss in purchasing power of the monetary assets borne by the owners.

CHAPTER 12

PROPERTY, PLANT, AND EQUIPMENT (IAS 16)

PROBLEMS ADDRESSED

The following aspects of accounting for property, plant, and equipment are prescribed:
- Timing of recognition of the assets.
- Determination of their carrying amounts.
- Depreciation charges to be recognized in relation to these values.
- Disclosure requirements.

12.2 SCOPE OF THE STANDARD

The standard deals with all property, plant, and equipment. Property, plant, and equipment are tangible assets held by an enterprise for use in production, supply of goods or services, rental, or administration purposes, and are expected to be used during more than one period. Examples include land, buildings, machinery, ships, aircraft, motor vehicles, furniture, and fittings.

12.3 ACCOUNTING TREATMENT

12.3.1 Property, plant, and equipment could be recorded on the following bases:
- Cost less accumulated depreciation and accumulated impairment losses; i.e., carrying amount/book value (**benchmark treatment**).
- Revalued amount (**allowed alternative**), which is its fair value less accumulated depreciation and accumulated impairment losses.

12.3.2 In certain jurisdictions, the annual depreciation charge for an item of property, plant, and equipment would differ from the depreciation deduction allowed by the taxation authorities. This would result in a difference between the carrying amount and the tax base of the item; deferred taxation should therefore be provided in terms of IAS 12.

12.3.3 An item of property, plant, and equipment is recognized as an asset in terms of the IAS Framework if:
- It is **probable** that the future economic benefits of the asset will flow to the enterprise (e.g., revenue from the sales of products produced by the asset).
- The cost of the asset should be **measured reliably** from the transaction itself (e.g., an invoice).

12.3.4 The following principles are applied for combining or separating assets:
- Insignificant items (e.g., molds and dies) could be aggregated as single asset items.
- Specialized spares and servicing equipment are accounted for as property, plant, and equipment.
- Component parts are treated as separate items if the related assets have different useful lives or provide economic benefits in a different pattern (e.g., an aircraft and its engines).
- Safety and environmental assets qualify as property, plant, and equipment if they enable the enterprise to increase future economic benefits from related assets in excess of what it could derive if they had not been acquired (e.g., chemical protection equipment).

12.3.5 A property, plant, and equipment item is measured at its directly attributable costs, including the purchase price and duties paid. However, general and administrative expenses as well as start-up costs are excluded.

12.3.6 The cost of self-constructed assets include materials, labor, and other inputs.

12.3.7 When assets are exchanged, dissimilar items are recorded at the fair value of the asset(s) received. Similar items are recorded at the carrying amount of the asset(s) given up.

12.3.8 Subsequent expenditure on property, plant, and equipment is recognized as an expense when incurred if it restores the performance standard. These are capitalized when it is probable that economic benefits in **excess** of the original standard of performance will flow to the enterprise *(SIC–23)*.

12.3.9 Depreciation reflects the consumption of economic benefits of an asset and is recognized as an expense unless it is included in the carrying amount of a self-constructed asset. The following principles apply:
- The depreciable amount is allocated on a systematic basis over the useful life.
- The method reflects the pattern of expected consumption. It includes the straight line, diminishing balance, and sum-of-the-units method.

12.3.10 Land and buildings are separable assets. Buildings are depreciable assets.

12.3.11 The amount expected to be recovered from the future use of an asset, including its residual value on disposal, is referred to as the **recoverable amount**. The carrying amount should be compared periodically (usually at year-end) with the recoverable amount. If the latter is lower, the difference is recognized as an expense unless it reverses a corresponding amount in the revaluation surplus.

12.4   DISCLOSURE

12.4.1 The main disclosure requirements include:

Accounting policies
- Measurement bases for **each** class of asset.
- Depreciation methods and rates for **each** class of asset.

Income statement and notes
- Depreciation charge for each class of asset.
- Effect of material changes in estimates of related costs of property, plant, and equipment items.

Balance sheet and notes
- Gross carrying amount (book value) less accumulated depreciation and accumulated impairment losses for **each** class of asset at the beginning and end of the period.
- Detailed reconciliation of movements in the carrying amount during the period.
- Amount of property, plant, and equipment in the course of construction.
- Property, plant, and equipment pledged as security.
- Capital commitments for acquisition of property, plant, and equipment.

12.4.2 **Additional** disclosures required for revalued amounts are as follows:
- The basis used and effective date of the revaluation.
- Balance of revaluation surplus.
- If an independent valuer was involved.
- Nature of any indices used to determine replacement costs.
- Carrying amount of **each** class property, plant, and equipment had it been carried in the financial statements on the historical costs basis.

-- CASE STUDY --

PROPERTY, PLANT, AND EQUIPMENT

The following unrelated situations address accounting issues with regards to property, plant, and equipment where the balance sheet date is 31 December 20x1:

A.   On 1 January 20x1, Zakharetz Inc. acquired production equipment in the amount of $250,000. The following further costs were incurred:

	$
• Delivery	18,000
• Installation	24,500
• General administration costs of an indirect nature	3,000

The installation and setting-up period took 3 months, and a further amount of $21,000 was spent on start-up costs directly related to bringing the asset to its working condition.

Monthly managerial reports indicated that for the first 5 months, the production quantities from this equipment resulted in an initial operating loss of $15,000 because of small quantities produced. The months thereafter show much more positive results.

The equipment has an estimated useful life of 14 years and a residual value of $18,000. Estimated dismantling costs amount to $12,500.

ISSUES: What value is originally recorded as the historical cost of the asset and what are the annual charges in the income statement related to the consumption of the economic benefits embodied in the assets?

Historical cost of equipment

	$
Invoice price	250,000
Delivery	18,000
Installation	24,500
Start-up costs	21,000
	313,500

Annual charges related to equipment

	$
Historical cost above	313,500
Estimated residual value	(18,000)
Estimated dismantling costs	12,500
Depreciable amount	308,000

The annual charge to the income statement is $22,000 (308,000 ÷ 14 yrs). However, note that in the year ending 31 December 20x1, the charge will be $16,500 (9/12 x $22,000) because the equipment was taken into use on 1 April 20x1, after the installation and setting-up period.

CASE STUDY

CONTINUED

PROPERTY, PLANT, AND EQUIPMENT

B.   Delta Printers Inc. acquired its buildings and printing machinery on 1 January 20x1 for the amount of $2 million and recorded it at the historical cost. During 20x3, the directors made a decision to account for the machinery at fair value in the future, to provide for the maintenance of capital of the business in total.

ISSUES: Will measurement at fair value achieve the objective of capital maintenance?

How is fair value determined?

What are the deferred tax implications?

Maintenance of capital

The suggested method of accounting treatment will not be completely successful for the maintenance of capital due to the following:

- No provision is made for maintaining the current cost of inventory, work-in-process, and other non-monetary assets.
- No provision is made for the cost of holding monetary assets.
- No provision is made for back-log depreciation.

Fair value

- The fair value of **land and buildings** is usually the market value for current use, which assumes the continuous use of the asset in the same or similar operation. The value is determined through valuation, usually done by a professional valuer.
- The fair value of **plant and equipment items** are usually their market value determined by appraisal. When there is no proof of market value, due to the specialized nature of plant and equipment and because these items are rarely sold (except as part of a going concern), then the items are to be valued at net replacement cost.
- The calculation of a fair value of property, plant, and equipment is usually based on **existing use**. For an asset in which change in use is probable, the fair value is calculated on the same basis as other similar assets that are used for the same **intended purpose**.

Deferred tax implication of revaluation

- Deferred taxation is provided for on the revaluation amount even when the revaluation is above the cost price and the entity has no intention of selling the assets.
- The revalued carrying amount is then recovered through use, and taxable economic benefits are obtained against which no depreciation deductions for tax purposes are allowed. Therefore, the taxation payable on these economic benefits should be provided.
- Deferred taxation, as a result of revaluation, is provided for directly against the revaluation surplus (equity).

CHAPTER 13

LEASES (IAS 17)

13.1 PROBLEMS ADDRESSED

The IAS describes, for **lessees** and **lessors**, the appropriate accounting policies and disclosure that should be applied to various types of lease transactions.

13.2 SCOPE OF THE STANDARD

This standard applies to all lease agreements, whereby the lessor conveys to the lessee in return for a payment or series of payments the right to use an asset for an agreed period of time. *SIC–15 clarifies the recognition of incentives related to operating leases by both the lessee and lessor.*

13.3 ACCOUNTING TREATMENT

13.3.1 A distinction is made between the two types of lease arrangements:
- **Finance leases**, which transfer substantially all the risks and rewards incident to ownership of an asset. Title may or may not eventually be transferred.
- **Operating leases**, which are leases other than finance leases.

13.3.2 The classification of leases is done at inception of lease. The **substance** rather than the **form** of the lease contract is indicative of the classification. The classification is based on the extent to which risks and rewards incident to ownership of a leased asset lie with the lessor or the lessee.
- **Risks** include potential losses from idle capacity, technological obsolescence, and variations in return due to changing economic conditions.
- **Rewards** include the expectation of profitable operation over the asset's economic life and of gain from appreciation in value or the realization of a residual value.

13.3.3 Finance leases include the following:
- Lease transfers ownership of asset to the lessee at the expiration of the lease.
- Lessee has a bargain purchase option that will be exercised with reasonable certainty.
- Lease term is for a major part of the economic life of the asset.
- Present value of minimum lease payments approximates fair value of the leased asset.
- Leased assets is of a specialized nature and only suitable for lessee.
- Lessee will bear cancellation losses.
- Fluctuation gains/losses of residual value passed on to lessee.
- Lease for secondary period possible at substantial lower-than-market rent.

ACCOUNTING BY LESSEES

13.3.4 An asset held under a **finance lease** and the corresponding obligation are recognized in terms of the principle of **substance over form**. The accounting treatment is as follows:
- At inception, the asset and corresponding liability for future lease payments are recognized at the same amounts.
- Initial direct costs in connection with lease activities are capitalized to the asset.
- Lease payments consist of the finance charge and the reduction of the outstanding liability. Finance charge to be a constant periodic rate of interest on the remaining balance of the liability for each period.

- Depreciation is recognized in terms of IAS 16 and IAS 38.

13.3.5 Operating lease payments (excluding costs for services such as insurance) are recognized as an expense in the income statement on a straight line basis, or a systematic basis that is representative of the time pattern of the user's benefit, even if the payments are not on that basis.

ACCOUNTING BY LESSORS

13.3.6 An asset held under a **finance lease** is presented as a receivable. It is accounted for as follows:
- The receivable is recorded at the net investment.
- The recognition of finance income is based on a pattern reflecting a constant periodic rate of return on the net investment.
- Initial direct costs are either recognized immediately or allocated against finance income over the lease term.

13.3.7 An **operating leased** asset is classified according to its nature. It is accounted for as follows:
- Depreciation is recognized in terms of IAS 16 and IAS 38.
- Lease income is recognized on a straight line basis over the lease term, unless another systematic basis is more representative.
- Initial direct costs are either recognized immediately or allocated against rent income over the lease term.

SALE AND LEASEBACK TRANSACTIONS

13.3.8 If the leaseback is a **finance lease**, any excess of sales proceeds over the carrying amount in the books of the lessee (vendor) should be deferred and amortized over the lease term. The transaction is a means whereby the lessor **provides finance** to the lessee. It is therefore inappropriate to recognize the profit as income immediately.

13.3.9 Profit/loss from an **operating lease** concluded at fair value is recognized immediately. Transactions below or above fair value are recorded as follows:
- If the fair value is less than the carrying amount of the asset, a loss equal to the difference is recognized immediately.
- If the sale price is above fair value, the excess over fair value should be deferred and amortized over the lease period.
- If the sale price is below fair value, any profit/loss is recognized immediately unless a loss is compensated by future lease payments at below market price; in this case, the loss should be deferred and amortized in proportion to the lease payments.

13.4 DISCLOSURE

13.4.1 LESSEES
Finance leases
- Asset: carrying amount of **each** class of asset.
- Liability: total of minimum lease payments reconciled to the present values of lease liabilities in **three periodic bands**, namely:
  - Not later than 1 year.
  - Not later than 5 years.
  - Later than 5 years.
- IAS 16 requirements for leased property, plant, and equipment.
- General description of significant leasing arrangements.

- Distinction between current and non-current lease liabilities.
- Future minimum sublease payments expected to be received under non-cancellable subleases at balance sheet date.
- Contingent rents recognized in income for the period.

Operating leases

- General description of significant leasing arrangements (same information as for finance leases above).
- Lease and sublease payments recognized in income of the current period, separating minimum lease payments, contingent rents, and sublease payments.
- Future minimum non-cancellable lease payments in the **three periodic bands.**
- Future minimum sublease payments expected to be received under non-cancellable subleases at balance sheet date.

13.4.2 LESSORS

Finance leases

- The total gross investment reconciled to the present value of minimum lease payments receivable in the **three periodic bands**.
- Unearned finance income.
- Accumulated allowance for uncollectible receivables.
- Contingent rents recognized in income.
- General description of significant leasing arrangements.
- Unguaranteed residual values.

Operating leases

- All related disclosure under IAS 16, IAS 36, IAS 38 and IAS 40.
- General description of significant leasing arrangements.
- Total future minimum lease payments under non-cancellable operating leases in **the three periodic bands.**
- Total contingent rents recognized in income.

13.4.3 SALE AND LEASEBACK TRANSACTIONS

- Same disclosures for lessees and lessors apply.
- Some items may be separately disclosable in terms of IAS 8.

─────────── CASE STUDY ───────────

LEASES

A manufacturing machine with a cash price of $330,000 is acquired by way of a finance lease agreement under the following terms:

- Effective date: 1 January 20x2
- Lease term: 3 years
- Installments of $72,500 are payable half-yearly in arrears
- Effective rate of interest is 23.5468 percent per annum
- Deposit of $30,000 immediately payable.

The amortization table for this transaction would be as follows:

	Installment	Interest	Capital	Balance
	$	$	$	$
Cash price				330,000
Deposit	30,000	–	30,000	300,000
Installment 1	72,500	35,320	37,180	262,820
Installment 2	72,500	30,943	41,557	221,263
Subtotal	175,000	66,263	108,737	
Installment 3	72,500	26,050	46,450	174,813
Installment 4	72,500	20,581	51,919	122,894
Installment 5	72,500	14,469	58,031	64,863
Installment 6	72,500	7,637	64,863	–
TOTAL	**465,000**	**135,000**	**330,000**	

The finance lease would be recognized and presented in the financial statements as follows:

BOOKS OF THE LESSEE
An asset of $330,000 will be recorded and a corresponding liability would be raised on 1 January 20x2.

If it is assumed that the machine is depreciated on a straight-line basis over a period of six years, the following expenses would be recognized in the **income statement** for the first year:

- Depreciation (330,000 ÷ 6) $55,000
- Finance lease charges (35,320 + 30,943) $66,263

The **balance sheet** at 31 December 20x2 would reflect the following balances:
- Machine (330,000 – 55,000) $275,000 Dr
- Long-term finance lease liability $221,263 Cr

CASE STUDY

CONTINUED

LEASES

BOOKS OF THE LESSOR

The gross amount of $465,000 due by the lessee, would be recorded as a debtor at inception of the contract, i.e., the deposit of $30,000 plus six installments of $72,500 each. The unearned finance income of $135,000 is recorded as a deferred income (credit balance). The net amount reflected would then be $330,000 ($465,000 – $135,000).

The deposit as well as the first two installments are credited to the debtor account, which will then reflect a debit balance of $290,000 at 31 December 20x2.

A total of $66,263 ($35,320 + $30,943) of the unearned finance income has been earned in the first year, which brings the balance of this account to $68,737 at 31 December 20x2.

The **income statement** for the year ending 31 December 20x2 would reflect finance income earned in the first year to an amount of $66,263.

The **balance sheet** at 31 December 20x2 will reflect the net investment as a long-term receivable at $221,263 ($290,000 – $68,737), which agrees with the liability in the books of the lessor at that stage.

CHAPTER 14

REVENUE (IAS 18)

14.1 PROBLEMS ADDRESSED

The accounting treatment of revenue arising from **ordinary activities** is described. The following aspects are addressed:

- Revenue is distinguished from other income. (Income includes both revenue and gains.)
- Recognition criteria for revenue is identified.
- Practical guidance is provided on:
  - Moment of recognition.
  - Amount to be recognized.
  - Disclosure requirements.

14.2 SCOPE OF THE STANDARD

The IAS deals with the accounting treatment of revenue that comes from:

- Sale of goods.
- Rendering of services.
- Use by others of enterprise assets yielding interest, royalties, and dividends.

Revenue is the gross inflow of economic benefits:

- during the period,
- arising in ordinary course of activities,
- resulting in increases in equity, other than contributions by equity participants.

Revenue excludes amounts collected on behalf of third parties, e.g., VAT.

14.3 ACCOUNTING TREATMENT

14.3.1 Revenue should be measured at the **fair value** of the consideration **received**:

- Trade discounts and volume rebates are deducted to determine fair value. However, payment discounts are non-deductible.
- When the inflow of cash is deferred (e.g., the provision of interest free credit), it effectively constitutes a financing transaction. The imputed rate of interest should be calculated. The difference between the fair value and nominal amount of the consideration is separately recognized and disclosed as interest.
- When goods or services are exchanged for that of a similar nature and value, no revenue recognition occurs.
- When goods or services are rendered in exchange for dissimilar goods or services, revenue is measured at the fair value of the goods or services **received**.

14.3.2 Rules for the identification of transactions that generate revenue are as follows:

- When the selling price of a product includes an amount for subsequent servicing, that amount is deferred over the period that the service is performed.
- When an enterprise sells goods and immediately concludes an agreement to repurchase them at a later date, the substantive effect of the transaction is negated and the two transactions are dealt with as one.

14.3.3 Revenue from the sale of goods is recognized when:
- Significant risks and rewards of ownership of the goods is transferred to the buyer.
- The enterprise retains neither continuing managerial involvement of ownership nor effective control over the goods sold.
- The amount of revenue can be measured reliably.
- It is probable that the economic benefits of the transaction will flow to the enterprise.
- The costs of the transaction can be measured reliably.

14.3.4 Uncertainty about the collectability of an amount already included in revenue is treated as an expense rather than as an adjustment to revenue.

14.3.5 Revenue cannot be recognized when the expenses cannot be measured reliably. Consideration already received for the sale is deferred as a liability until revenue recognition can take place.

14.3.6 When the outcome of a transaction involving the rendering of services can be **estimated reliably**, revenue is recognized by reference to the **stage of completion** of the transaction at **balance sheet date**. The outcome can be estimated when:
- The amount of revenue can be measured reliably.
- It is probable that the economic benefits of the transaction will flow to the enterprise.
- The stage of completion can be measured reliably.
- The costs incurred and the costs to complete the transaction can be measured reliably.

14.3.7 When the outcome of the transaction involving the rendering of services **cannot be estimated reliably**, revenue should be recognized only to the extent of the expenses that are recoverable.

14.3.8 The **stage of completion** of a transaction may be determined by a variety of methods similar to that described in IAS 11 (e.g., the proportion of costs incurred to total estimated costs; see paragraph 8.3.6).

14.3.9 Revenue arising from the use by others of enterprise assets yielding interest, royalties, and dividends should be recognized as follows:
- **Interest**: Time proportion basis (principal amount outstanding, %, time).
- **Royalties**: Accrual basis (substance of the relevant agreements).
- **Dividends**: When the right to receive payment is established.

14.4   DISCLOSURE

Accounting policies
- Revenue measurement bases used.
- Revenue recognition methods used.
- Stage of completion method for services.

Income statement and notes
- Amounts of significant revenue categories:
  - Sale of goods.
  - Rendering of services.
  - Interest.
  - Royalties.
  - Dividends.
- Amount of revenue recognized from the exchange of goods or services.

CASE STUDY

REVENUE

A generous benefactor donates raw materials to an enterprise for use in its production process. The materials had cost the benefactor $20,000 and had a market value of $30,000 at the time of donation. The materials are still on hand at the balance sheet date. No entry has been made in the books of the enterprise. The question is whether the donation should be recognized as revenue in the books of the enterprise.

The proper accounting treatment of the above matter is as follows:

- The accounting standard that deals with inventories, IAS 2, provides no guidance on the treatment of inventory acquired by donation. However, donations received meet the definition of **revenue** in IAS 18 (i.e., the gross inflow of economic benefits during the period arising in the course of ordinary activities when those inflows result in increases in equity, other than increases relating to contributions from equity participants). It could be argued that receiving a donation is not part of the **ordinary course of activities**. In such a case the donation would be regarded as a capital gain. For purposes of this case study, the donation is regarded as revenue.

- The donations should be recorded as revenue measured at its fair value ($30,000) of the raw materials received (as that is the economic benefit).

- The debit clearly meets the Framework's definition of an asset, because the raw materials (**resource**) is now owned (**controlled**) by the corporation as a result of the donation (**past event**) from which a profit can be made in the future (**future economic benefits**); see paragraph 2.3.6. The recognition criteria of the Framework, namely those of measurability and probability, are also satisfied; see paragraph 2.3.8.

- As the debit coming from the donation relates to trading items, it should be disclosed as inventory, with the fair value of $30,000 at the acquisition date being treated as the cost thereof.

CHAPTER 15

EMPLOYEE BENEFITS (IAS 19)

The standard prescribes the accounting recognition and measurement principles as well as the disclosure requirements for employee benefits.

15.2   SCOPE OF THE STANDARD

The IAS applies to all employee benefits including those provided under both formal arrangements and informal practices. Five types of employee benefits are identified, namely:

- Short-term employee benefits (e.g., bonuses, wages, and social security).
- Post-employment benefits (e.g., pensions and other retirement benefits).
- Other long-term employee benefits (e.g., long-service leave and, if not due within 12 months, profit sharing, bonuses, and deferred compensation).
- Termination benefits.
- Equity compensation benefits (e.g., employee share options).

15.3   ACCOUNTING TREATMENT

15.3.1   Employee benefits may be provided in terms of both the following:

- **Legal obligations**, which arise from the operation of law (e.g., agreements and plans between the enterprise and employees or their representatives).
- **Constructive obligations**, which arise from informal practices that result in an obligation whereby the enterprise has no realistic alternative but to pay employee benefits (e.g., the enterprise has a history of increasing benefits for former employees to keep pace with inflation even if there is no legal obligation to do so).

15.3.2   Two types of post-employment benefit plans are distinguished, namely:

- **Defined contribution plan**: The enterprise's legal or constructive obligation is limited to the amount it agrees to contribute to the fund. The actuarial risk (that assets invested will be insufficient to meet expected benefits) falls on the employee.
- **Defined benefit plan**: The enterprise's obligation is to provide the agreed benefits to current and former employees. Actuarial risk (that benefits will cost more than expected) and investment risk fall on the enterprise.

SHORT-TERM EMPLOYEE BENEFITS

15.3.3   These should be recognized as an expense when the employee has rendered services in exchange for the benefits **or** when the enterprise has a legal or constructive obligation to make such payments as a result of past events, e.g., profit sharing plans.

POST-EMPLOYMENT BENEFITS
Under defined contribution plans

15.3.4   An enterprise recognizes contributions to a defined contribution plan as an expense when an employee has rendered services in exchange for those contributions. When the contributions do not fall due within 12 months after the accounting period that services were rendered, they should be discounted.

Under defined benefit plans

15.3.5 The following rules apply:
- An enterprise determines the present value of defined benefit **obligations** and the fair value of any **plan assets** with sufficient regularity that the amounts recognized in the financial statements do not differ materially from the amounts that would be determined at the **balance sheet date**.
- An enterprise should use the **projected unit credit method** to measure the present value of its defined benefit obligations and related current and past service costs. This method sees each period of service as giving rise to an additional unit of benefit entitlement and measures each unit separately to build up the final obligation.
- Unbiased and mutually compatible actuarial assumptions about demographic variables (e.g., employee turnover and mortality) and financial variables (e.g., future increases in salaries and certain changes in benefits) should be used.
- The difference between the fair value of any plan assets and the carrying amount of the defined benefit obligation is recognized as a liability or an asset.
- When it is virtually certain that another party will reimburse some or all of the expenditure required to settle a defined benefit obligation, an enterprise should recognize its right to reimbursement as a separate asset.
- Offsetting of assets and liabilities of different plans are not allowed.
- The net total of current service cost, interest cost, expected return on plan assets and on any reimbursement rights, actuarial gains and losses, past service cost and the effect of any plan curtailments or settlements should be recognized as expense or income.
- Recognize past service cost on a straight-line basis over the average period until the amended benefits become vested.
- Recognize gains or losses on the curtailment or settlement of a defined benefit plan when the curtailment or settlement occurs.
- Recognize a specified portion of the net cumulative actuarial gains and losses that exceed the **greater** of:
  - 10% of the present value of the defined benefit obligation (before deducting plan assets), and
  - 10% of the fair value of any plan assets.

  The minimum portion to be recognized for each defined benefit plan is the excess that falls outside the 10% 'corridor' at the previous reporting date, divided by the expected average remaining working lives of the employees participating in that plan. Earlier recognition of these gains and losses is permitted.

OTHER LONG-TERM BENEFITS

15.3.6 Virtually the same rules apply as for defined benefit plans. However, a more simplified method of accounting is required for actuarial gains and losses as well as past service costs, which are recognized immediately.

TERMINATION BENEFITS

15.3.7 The event that results in an obligation is termination rather than employee service. An enterprise should therefore recognize termination benefits only when it is demonstrably committed through a detailed formal plan to either:
- terminate the employment of an employee or group of employees before the normal retirement date, **or**

- provide termination benefits as a result of an offer made in order to encourage voluntary redundancy.

Termination benefits falling due more than 12 months after balance sheet date should be discounted.

EQUITY COMPENSATION BENEFITS

15.3.8 No recognition or measurement requirements are specified; only disclosure requirements are specified.

15.4   DISCLOSURE

The **main** disclosure requirements are:

Accounting policies

- Methods applied for the recognition of the various types of employee benefits.
- Description of post-employment benefit plans.
- Description of equity compensation plans.
- Actuarial valuation methods used.
- Principal actuarial assumptions.

Income statement and notes

- Expense recognized for contribution plans.
- Expense recognized for benefit plans and the line items in which they are included.
- Expense recognized for equity compensation plans.

Balance sheet and notes

- Details about the recognized defined benefit assets and liabilities.
- Reconciliation of the movements of the aforementioned.
- Amounts included in the fair value of plan assets in respect of:
  - The enterprise's own financial instruments.
  - Property occupied or assets used by the enterprise.
- The actual return on plan assets.
- Liability raised for equity compensation plans.
- Financial instruments issued to and held by equity compensation plans as well as the fair values thereof.
- Share options held by and exercised under equity compensation plans.

CASE STUDY

Employee Benefits

On 31 December 20x0, an enterprise's balance sheet includes a pension liability of $12 million. Management has made the decision to adopt IAS 19 as of 1 January 20x1 for the purpose of accounting for employee benefits. At that date, the present value of the obligation under IAS 19 is calculated at $146 million and the fair value of plan assets is determined at $110 million. On 1 January 19x6, the enterprise had improved pension benefits (cost for non-vested benefits amounted to $16 million; and the average remaining period at that date, until vesting, was 8 years).

The transitional liability is calculated as follows:

	$ million
Present value of the obligation	146
Fair value of plan assets	(110)
Past service cost to be recognized in later periods (16 x 3/8)	(6)
Transitional liability	30
Liability already recognized	12
Increase in liability	18

The enterprise may (in terms of the transitional provisions of IAS 19) choose to recognize the transitional liability of $18 million either immediately or recognize it as an expense on a straight-line basis up to 5 years. The choice is irrevocable.

CHAPTER 16

ACCOUNTING FOR GOVERNMENT GRANTS AND DISCLOSURE OF GOVERNMENT ASSISTANCE (IAS 20)

16.1 PROBLEMS ADDRESSED

IAS 20 addresses the following aspects of accounting for government grants and other forms of government assistance:

- Accounting treatment.
- Disclosure of the extent of the benefit(s) recognized or received in each accounting period.
- Disclosure of other forms of government assistance.

16.2 SCOPE OF THE STANDARD

The IAS should be applied to account for:

- **Government grants**: Transfers of resources to an enterprise by government in return for past or future compliance with conditions relating to the operating activities.
  SIC–10 states that even a general requirement to operate in certain regions or industry sectors would constitute such a condition.
- **Government assistance**: Action by government to provide a specific economic benefit for an entity(ies). It excludes benefits provided indirectly through action affecting general trading conditions (e.g., provision of infrastructure).

16.3 ACCOUNTING TREATMENT

16.3.1 The term **government** refers to government, government agencies, and similar bodies whether local, national, or international. The following distinction is made between the two types of government grants:

- **Grants related to assets**: Grants whereby an enterprise qualifying for them should purchase, construct, or otherwise acquire long-term assets.
- **Grants related to income**: Government grants other than those related to assets.

16.3.2 The two broad approaches of accounting are:

- **Capital approach**: A grant is credited directly to shareholder's interest because no repayment is required, and it is not earned.
- **Income approach**: A grant is recognized in income over one or more periods, since it is not contributed by shareholders and should be **matched** with costs that the grant is intended to compensate.
  The latter approach is required by IAS 20.

16.3.3 **Government grants** should be accounted for as follows:

- Government grants, including non-monetary grants at fair value, should only be recognized when there is **reasonable assurance** that:
  - The enterprise will comply with the conditions attached to them.
  - The grants will be received.
- A grant received in cash or as a reduction of a liability to government is accounted for similarly.

65

- A forgivable loan (where the lender undertakes to waive repayment of loans under prescribed conditions) is treated as a grant when there is reasonable assurance that the terms for forgiveness of the loan will be met.
- Government grants should be recognized as income and not be credited directly to equity. The income is recognized on a systematic basis over the periods necessary to **match** them with related costs that they should compensate. Examples include:
  - Grants related to depreciable assets recognized as income over the periods and in the proportions to which depreciation is charged.
  - A grant of land may be conditional upon the erection of a building on the site. Income is normally then recognized over the life of the building.
- A government grant as compensation for expenses or losses already incurred or immediate financial support with no future related costs is recognized as income of the period in which it becomes receivable.
- Non-monetary grants (e.g., land or other resources) is assessed and recorded at fair value. Alternatively, the grant and asset(s) are recorded at a nominal amount.
- A repayment of a government grant is accounted for as a revision of an accounting estimate (refer to IAS 8) as follows:
  - Repayment related to income is first applied against an unamortized deferred grant credit.
  - Repayment in excess of a deferred grant credit is recognized as an expense.
  - Repayment related to an asset is recorded by increasing the carrying amount of the asset or reducing a deferred income balance. (Cumulative additional depreciation that would have been recognized to date is recognized immediately.)

16.3.4 **Government assistance** includes:
- Free technical and marketing advice.
- Provision of guarantees.
- Government procurement policy that is responsible for a portion of the enterprise's sales.
- Loans at nil or low interest rates (the benefit is not quantified by the imputation of interest).

16.4   PRESENTATION & DISCLOSURE
16.4.1 PRESENTATION
- Asset-related grants: Present in the **balance sheet**, either by:
  - setting up the grant as deferred income, or
  - deducting it from the carrying amount of the asset.
- Income-related grants: Present in the **income statement**, either as:
  - separate credit line item, or
  - deduction from the related expense.

16.4.2 DISCLOSURE
Accounting policies
- Method of presentation.
- Method of recognition.

Income statement and notes
- Government grants:
  - Nature.
  - Extent/amount.
- Government assistance:
  - Nature.
  - Extent.
  - Duration.
- Unfulfilled conditions.
- Contingencies attached to assistance.

─── CASE STUDY ───

ACCOUNTING FOR GOVERNMENT GRANTS AND DISCLOSURE OF GOVERNMENT ASSISTANCE

Uyanik Inc. obtained a grant of $10,000,000 from a government agency for an investment project to construct a manufacturing plant of at least $88,000,000. The principal term is that the grant payments relate to the level of capital expenditure. The secondary intention of the grant is to safeguard 500 jobs. The grant will have to be repaid pro rata if there is an underspending on capital. Twenty percent of the grant will have to be repaid if the jobs are not safeguarded until 18 months after the date of the last asset purchase.

The plant was completed on 1 January 20x4 at a total cost of $90,000,000 The plant has an expected useful life of 20 years and is depreciated on a straight-line basis with no residual value.

The grant should be recognized as income on a systematic basis over the periods that will match it with related costs that it is intended to compensate.

Difficulties may arise where the terms of the grant do not specify precisely the expenditure to which it is intended to contribute. Grants may be received to cover costs comprising both capital and revenue expenditure. This would require a detailed analysis of the terms of the grant.

The employment condition should be seen as an additional condition to prevent replacement of labor by capital, rather than as the reason for the grant. This grant should therefore be regarded as an **asset-related grant**. IAS 20 allows two acceptable methods of presentation of such grants. The application of each method is demonstrated for the first three years of operation:

i.   **Setting grant up as deferred income**

The plant would be reflected as follows in the balance sheets at 31 December of the years as indicated:

	20x6	20x5	20x4
	$'000	$'000	$'000
Plant			
• Historical cost	90,000	90,000	90,000
• Accumulated depreciation	(13,500)	(9,000)	(4,500)
	76,500	81,000	85,500

The following amounts would be recognized in the income statements of the respective years:

	20x6	20x5	20x4
	$'000	$'000	$'000
Depreciation (expense) (90,000,000 ÷ 20)	4,500	4,500	4,500
Government grant (income) (10,000,000 ÷ 20)	(500)	(500)	(500)

The above amounts are treated as separate income statement items and should not be off-set under this method of presentation.

--------------------- CASE STUDY ---------------------

CONTINUED

ACCOUNTING FOR GOVERNMENT GRANTS AND DISCLOSURE OF GOVERNMENT ASSISTANCE

ii.   Deducting grant in arriving at carrying amount of asset

The adjusted historical cost of the plant would be $80 million, which is the total cost of $90 million less the $10 million grant.

The plant would be reflected as follows in the respective balance sheets:

	20x6 $'000	20x5 $'000	20x4 $'000
Plant			
• Historical cost	80,000	80,000	80,000
• Accumulated depreciation	(12,000)	(8,000)	(4,000)
	68,000	72,000	76,000

The income statements would reflect an annual depreciation charge of $4,000,000 ($80,000,000 ÷ 20). This charge agrees with the net result of the annual amounts recognized in the income statement under the first alternative.

CHAPTER 17

THE EFFECTS OF CHANGES IN FOREIGN EXCHANGE RATES (IAS 21)

17.1 PROBLEMS ADDRESSED

The accounting treatment for foreign currency transactions and foreign operations is prescribed. The principle aspects addressed are:

- Which exchange rate(s) should be used for recording and translation purposes?
- How to recognize the financial effect of changes in exchange rates in financial statements.

17.2 SCOPE OF THE STANDARD

The IAS should be applied to account for:

- Foreign currency transactions.
- Translation of the financial statements of foreign operations.

17.3 ACCOUNTING TREATMENT

FOREIGN CURRENCY TRANSACTIONS

17.3.1 Foreign currency transactions are transactions denominated in a foreign currency, including:

- Buying or selling of goods or services.
- Borrowing or lending of funds.
- Concluding unperformed foreign exchange contracts.
- Acquiring or selling assets.
- Incurring or settling liabilities.

17.3.2 The following rules should be applied for the **recognition and measurement** of foreign currency transactions:

- Use the spot rate ruling at transaction date.
- If not settled in the same accounting period as incurred, the resultant monetary items (i.e., amounts to be received or paid in cash) are translated at the closing rate.
- Exchange differences on settlement of monetary items are recognized in income.
- Non-monetary items (e.g., inventories, property, plant, and equipment) carried at historical cost are reported at spot rate on transaction date.
- Non-monetary items carried at fair values are reported at spot rate on date of valuation.
- Exchange differences from the translation of monetary items at balance sheet date are recognized in income.
- In accordance with an **allowed alternative treatment**, exchange differences from a severe devaluation in a currency may under strict conditions be included in the carrying amount of assets; refer to *(SIC–11)*.
- Exchange differences arising from an **intragroup monetary item** that forms part of an enterprise's net investment in a foreign entity are included in equity until disposal.
- Exchange differences arising from **a foreign liability that serves as a hedge of an enterprise's net investment** in a foreign entity are included in equity until disposal.

FOREIGN OPERATIONS

17.3.3 A foreign operation is a subsidiary, associate, joint venture, or branch, the activities of which are based or conducted in a country other than the country of the reporting enterprise. Two types are distinguished:

- **Foreign entity**: Foreign operation, the activities of which are not an integral part of those of the reporting enterprise.
- **Integrated foreign operation**: Foreign operation that is integral to the operations of the reporting enterprise.

For classification purposes, various indicators are taken into account based on how the foreign operation is **financed** and **operates** in relation to the reporting enterprise. The method used for translating financial statements of foreign operations is based on its classification.

17.3.4 The **closing rate method** is used for the translation of the financial statements **of foreign entities**. The translation rules are:

- All assets and liabilities should be translated at closing rate (on balance sheet date).
- Income and expenses should be translated at actual transaction dates. Approximate or average rates are also allowed for practical reasons.
- Special rules apply to foreign entities in countries with hyperinflation.
- All resulting exchange differences are taken directly to equity (i.e., foreign currency translation reserve, FCTR).
- On disposal of the net investment, the total amount in FCTR is recognized in income.

17.3.5 The **temporal method** is used for the translation of the financial statements of **integrated foreign operations**. The items in the financial statements are translated as if all transactions of the foreign operation were entered into by the reporting entity itself. The translation rules are:

- All monetary items should be translated at closing rate.
- Non-monetary items recorded at historical cost are translated at historical rates.
- Non-monetary items held by the foreign operation at acquisition of the investment in such operation are translated at the rate on date of acquisition.
- Revalued non-monetary items are translated at rates on the dates of valuation.
- Components of owners' interest are translated at historical rates.
- Income statement items are translated at rates on the dates of the transactions or at any appropriate weighted average exchange rate for the period.
- Exchange differences are taken to income.
- Adjustments may be required in the group statements in terms of IAS 21.28 to reduce the carrying amount of an asset to recoverable amount or net realizable value.

17.3.6 A change in the classification of foreign operations may occur depending on the circumstances. The following translation procedures relating to the revised classification should be applied from the date of the change:

- **Integrated operation to a foreign entity**: Exchange differences from the translation on date of reclassification are taken to the FCTR.
- **Foreign entity to integrated operation**: The FCTR remains unchanged until the operation is sold. Non-monetary items are recorded at the rate on the date of the reclassification, which then becomes the "purchase date."

17.4 DISCLOSURE

Accounting policies

- Method to translate goodwill and fair value adjustments.
- Method to translate financial statements.
- State the reason if an alien reporting currency is used.
- Report a change in reporting currency.

Income statement

- The amount of foreign exchange differences included in the net profit or loss for the period.

Balance sheet

- Balance of the FCTR.

Notes

- A reconciliation of the opening and closing balance of the FCTR.
- For a change in the classification, state the nature, reason, impact on equity, and impact on net profit or loss for each period presented.
- The effect on foreign monetary items and on the financial statements of a foreign operation of significant changes in exchange rates occurring after balance sheet, in terms of IAS 10.

CASE STUDY

THE EFFECTS OF CHANGES IN FOREIGN EXCHANGE RATES

Bark Incorporated purchased manufacturing equipment from the United Kingdom. The transaction was financed by means of a loan from a bank in England.

Equipment that costs £400,000 was purchased on 2 January 20x7 and the loan amount was paid by the bank to the supplier on that same day. The loan must be repaid on 31 December 20x8 and interest is payable at 10 percent bi-annually in arrears. The balance sheet date is December 31.

The following exchange rates apply:

	£1 = $
2 January 20x7	1.67
30 June 20x7	1.71
31 December 20x7	1.75
30 June 20x8	1.73
31 December 20x8	1.70

The **interest payments** would be recorded at the spot rates applicable on the dates of payment in the following manner:

	$
30 June 20x7 (£20,000 x 1.71)	34,200
31 December 20x7 (£20,000 x 1.75)	35,000
Total interest for 20x7	69,200
30 June 20x8 (£20,000 x 1.73)	34,600
31 December 20x8 (£20,000 x 1.70)	34,000
Total interest for 20x8	68,600

The **loan** is initially recorded on 2 January 20x7 and restated at spot rate on 31 December 20x7 as well as 31 December 20x8, after which it is repaid at spot rate. The movements in the balance of the loan are reflected as follows:

	$
Recorded at 2 January 20x7 (£400,000 x 1.67)	668,000
Foreign currency loss on restatement of loan	32,000
Restate at 31 December 20x7 (£400,000 x 1.75)	700,000
Foreign currency profit on restatement of loan	(20,000)
Restate and pay at 31 December 20x8 (£400,000 x 1.70)	680,000

The loan will be stated at an amount of $700,000 in the **balance sheet** on 31 December 20x7.

The following amounts will be recognized in the **income statements**:

	20x8	20x7
	$	$
Interest	68,600	69,200
Foreign currency loss/(profit)	(20,000)	32,000

CHAPTER 18

BUSINESS COMBINATIONS (IAS 22)

18.1 PROBLEMS ADDRESSED

The standard prescribes the accounting treatment for business combinations. It is directed principally to a group of enterprises where the acquirer is the parent enterprise and the acquiree a subsidiary. The focus is on the accounting treatment **at date of acquisition**.

18.2 SCOPE OF THE STANDARD

The IAS should be applied in accounting for both types of business combinations, namely an **acquisition** of one enterprise by another, and the rare situation of a **uniting of interests** when an acquirer cannot be identified *(SIC–9)*.

18.3 ACCOUNTING TREATMENT

18.3.1 A business combination is the bringing together of separate enterprises into one economic entity as a result of one enterprise uniting with or obtaining control over the net assets and operations of another enterprise. Two types are identified:

- **Acquisition**: One of the enterprises (the acquirer) obtains control over the net assets and operations of another enterprise (the acquiree) in exchange for the transfer of assets, incurrence of a liability, or issue of equity.
- **Uniting of interests**: The shareholders of the combining enterprises combine control over their net assets and operations to achieve a continuing mutual sharing in the risks and benefits attaching to the combined entity such that neither party can be identified as the acquirer.

An acquisition is in substance different from a uniting of interests: the **substance rather than the form** of the transaction needs to be reflected in the financial statements; accordingly, a different accounting method is prescribed for each.

ACQUISITIONS

18.3.2 An acquisition should be accounted for by use of the **purchase method** of accounting. From the date of acquisition, an acquirer should:

- incorporate into the income statement the results of operations of the acquiree, and
- recognize in the balance sheet the identifiable assets and liabilities of the acquiree and any goodwill or negative goodwill arising from the acquisition.

18.3.3 The identifiable assets and liabilities acquired should be those of the acquiree that existed at the date of acquisition together with any liabilities arising from provisions for the termination or reduction of the activities of the acquiree (restructuring program).

18.3.4 **Two alternatives** are allowed for allocating the cost of acquisition:

- The identifiable assets and liabilities should be measured at the aggregate of their fair values at the date of the exchange transaction (to the extent of the acquirer's interest obtained in the exchange transaction) and the minority's proportion of their pre-acquisition carrying amounts.
- The identifiable assets and liabilities should be measured at their fair values at the date of acquisition. Any minority interest should be stated at the minority's proportion of their fair values.

18.3.5 The excess of the cost of acquisition over the acquirer's interest in the fair value of the identifiable assets and liabilities acquired is described as **goodwill** and recognized as an asset. The opposite case is described and recognized as **negative goodwill**.

18.3.6 Goodwill should be amortized on a systematic basis over its useful life. There is a rebuttable presumption that the useful life of goodwill will not exceed 20 years. The straight-line method is normally adopted unless another method is more appropriate. When the 20-year presumption is rebutted, the goodwill should be tested for impairment annually and the reason(s) for rebutting the presumption disclosed.

18.3.7 Negative goodwill is recognized as income as follows:
- To the extent that it relates to expectations of measurable future losses and expenses identified in the acquirer's plan, goodwill should be recognized as income when the identified future losses and expenses occur.
- To the extent that it does not relate to future losses and expenses, negative goodwill not exceeding the fair values of the non-monetary assets acquired should be recognized as income over the remaining average useful life of these assets. Negative goodwill in excess of the fair values of the non-monetary assets acquired should be recognized as income immediately.

18.3.8 The standard contains specific provisions about subsequent changes in the cost of acquisition or changes in the value of identifiable assets and liabilities, which may result in consequential changes in goodwill or negative goodwill *(SIC–22)*.

UNITING OF INTERESTS

18.3.9 A uniting of interests should be accounted for by using the **pooling of interests method**. The financial statement items of the combining enterprises for the period in which the combination occurs (and for any comparative periods disclosed) should be included in the financial statements of the combined enterprise as if they had been combined from the beginning of the earliest period presented.

18.3.10 Expenditures incurred in relation to a uniting of interests should immediately be recognized as expenses.

TRANSITIONAL PROVISIONS

18.3.11 The IAS prescribes transitional provisions based on the manner in which the reporting enterprise has recognized goodwill/negative goodwill in the past. It recommends retrospective application of the standard's requirements.

18.4 DISCLOSURE

18.4.1 ALL BUSINESS COMBINATIONS

The following disclosures are made in the period **during which** the combination has taken place.
- Names and descriptions of the combining enterprises.
- Method of accounting.
- Effective date of the combination.
- Any operations resulting from the business combination that the enterprise has decided to dispose of.
- Transitional provisions adopted in the first annual financial statements.

18.4.2 ACQUISITIONS

The following additional disclosures are made in the financial statements for the period **during which** the **acquisition** has taken place:

- The percentage of voting shares acquired
- The cost of acquisition and a description of the purchase consideration.
- If the fair values of the assets and liabilities or the purchase consideration can be determined only on a provisional basis, this should be stated and reasons given. **Subsequent adjustments** should be disclosed and explained.
- The aggregate amount of provisions for terminating or reducing the activities of an acquiree is disclosed for each individual business combination.

The accounting treatment for **goodwill** and **negative goodwill** should be disclosed:

- Regarding the period over which goodwill is amortized or negative goodwill recognized.
- If goodwill is amortized over more than 20 years, the evidence that rebuts the presumption that the useful life will not exceed 20 years.
- If goodwill is not amortized on the straight-line basis, the basis used and the reason why that basis is more appropriate than the straight-line basis.
- To the extent that negative goodwill is deferred in accordance with IAS 22.61, the nature, amount, and timing of the expected future losses and expenses.
- The line item in the income statement in which the amortization of goodwill or the recognition of negative goodwill is included.
- A detailed itemized reconciliation of the carrying amount of goodwill/negative goodwill at the beginning and end of the accounting period; *comparatives are not required.*
- Negative goodwill presented in the balance sheet as a deduction from goodwill.

18.4.3 UNITING OF INTERESTS

The following additional disclosures are made in the financial statements for the period **during which** the **uniting of interests** has taken place:

- Description and number of shares issued.
- Percentage of each enterprise's voting shares exchanged to effect the uniting of interests.
- Amounts of assets and liabilities contributed by each enterprise.
- Sales revenue, other operating revenues, extraordinary items, and the net profit or loss of each enterprise prior to the date of the combination that are included in the net profit or loss of the combined enterprise.

18.4.4 BUSINESS COMBINATIONS AFTER THE BALANCE SHEET DATE

- As much of the disclosures (as is practicable) mentioned above should be furnished for all business combinations effected after balance sheet date. If it is impracticable to disclose any of this information, this fact should be disclosed.

CASE STUDY

BUSINESS COMBINATIONS

H Ltd. acquired a 70% interest in the equity shares of F Ltd. for an amount of $750,000 at 1 January 20x1. The abridged balance sheets of both companies at the date of acquisition were as follows:

	H Ltd.	F Ltd.
	$000	$000
Identifiable assets	8,200	2,000
Investment in F Ltd.	750	–
	8,950	2,000
Equity	6,000	1,200
Identifiable liabilities	2,950	800
	8,950	2,000

The fair value of the identifiable assets of F Ltd. amounts to $2,800,000.

The cost of acquisition may be allocated as follows in terms of the acceptable treatments:

Equity analysis of F Limited

	Total	Benchmark		Alternative	
		H Ltd.	Minority	H Ltd.	Minority
	$'000	$'000	$'000	$'000	$'000
Equity	1,200	840	360	840	360
Revaluation reserve	800	560	240	560	–
	2,000	1,400	600	1,400	360
Investment		(750)		(750)	
Negative goodwill		650		650	

The abridged consolidated balance sheet at the date of acquisition will appear as follows:

	Benchmark	Alternative
	$'000	$'000
Assets	11,000[a]	10,760[b]
Shareholders' equity	6,000	6,000
Minority interest *(comment)*	600	360
Negative goodwill	650	650
Liabilities	3,750[c]	3,750[c]
	11,000	10,760

a = 8,200 + 2,800

b = 8,200 + 2,000 + 70% x 800

c = 2,950 + 800

COMMENT: *Under the alternative treatment, the minority interest is stated at its proportion of the **pre-acquisition** carrying amounts of the net assets of the subsidiary [30% x (2,000 – 800)] = R360,000.*

CHAPTER 19

BORROWING COSTS (IAS 23)

19.1 PROBLEMS ADDRESSED

The acquisition, construction, or production of some assets may take a substantial period. If borrowing costs are incurred during that period, it may be legitimate to regard these costs as forming part of the costs of getting such assets ready for their intended use or sale. The IAS prescribes the alternative accounting treatments of borrowing costs.

19.2 SCOPE OF THE STANDARD

The IAS should be applied in accounting for borrowing costs, which are interest and other costs incurred by an enterprise in connection with the borrowing of funds.

19.3 ACCOUNTING TREATMENT

19.3.1 Arguments for and against capitalization of borrowing costs are:

For capitalization:
- Borrowing costs form part of acquisition costs.
- Costs included in assets is matched against revenue of future periods.
- Results in better comparability between assets purchased and constructed.

Against capitalization:
- Attempts to link borrowing costs to a specific asset is arbitrary.
- Different financing methods may result in different amounts capitalized for the same asset.
- Expensing borrowing costs causes better comparable results.

19.3.2 **Qualifying assets** are those assets that require a substantial period of time to bring them to their intended use or saleable condition, for example:
- Inventories requiring a substantial period to bring them to a saleable condition.
- Other assets such as manufacturing plants, power generation facilities, and investment properties.

19.3.3 Two methods of accounting for borrowing costs are allowed:
- The **benchmark** treatment for borrowing costs dictates that they should be recognized as an expense in the period in which they are incurred.
- The **allowed alternative** dictates that they should be expensed when incurred, except to the extent that they are allowed to be capitalized. Borrowing costs directly attributable to the acquisition, construction, or production of a qualifying asset may be capitalized when:
  - it is **probable** that they will result in future economic benefits to the enterprise, and
  - the costs can be **measured reliably**.

  *SIC–2 requires capitalization to **all** qualifying assets and periods.*

19.3.4 Capitalization **commences** when:
- Expenditures on a qualifying asset are being incurred.
- Borrowing costs are being incurred.
- Activities necessary to prepare the asset for its intended sale or use are in progress.

19.3.5 Capitalization should **cease** when:
- The asset is materially ready for its intended use or sale.
- Active development is suspended for extended periods.
- Construction is completed in part and the completed part can be used independently (e.g., a business center).

19.3.6 Capitalization should **not cease**:
- When all of the components need to be completed before any part of the asset can be sold or used (e.g., a plant).
- For brief interruptions in activities.
- During periods when substantial technical and administrative work is being carried out.
- For delays that are inherent in the asset acquisition process (e.g., wines that need long periods of maturity).

19.3.7 The **amount to be capitalized** is the borrowing costs that could have been **avoided** if the expenditure on the qualifying asset had not been made:
- If funds are **specifically borrowed** to obtain a particular asset, the amount of borrowing costs qualifying for capitalization is the actual costs incurred during the period, less income earned on temporary investment of those borrowings.
- If funds are **borrowed generally** and used to obtain an asset, the amount of borrowing costs to be capitalized should be determined by applying the weighted average of the borrowing costs to the expenditure on that asset. The amount capitalized during a period should not exceed the amount of borrowing costs incurred during that period.

19.3.8 When the carrying value of an asset, inclusive of capitalized interest, exceeds the net realizable value, the asset should be written down to the latter value.

19.4 DISCLOSURE

The following should be disclosed:
- Accounting policy adopted for borrowing costs.
- Capitalization rate used to calculate capitalized borrowing costs.
- Total borrowing costs incurred with a distinction between:
  - Amount recognized as an expense.
  - Amount capitalized.

```
┌─────────────────────── CASE STUDY ───────────────────────┐
```

BORROWING COSTS

Morskoy Inc. is constructing a warehouse that will take about 18 months to complete. It began construction on 1 January 20x2. The following payments were made during 20x2:

	$
31 January	200,000
31 March	450,000
30 June	100,000
31 October	200,000
30 November	250,000

The first payment on 31 January was funded from the enterprise's pool of debt. However, the enterprise succeeded in raising a medium-term loan for an amount of $800,000 at 31 March 20x2 with simple interest of 9% per annum, calculated and payable monthly in arrears. These funds were specifically used for this construction. Excess funds were temporarily invested at 6% per annum monthly in arrears and payable in cash. The pool of debt was again used to an amount of $200,000 for the payment on 30 November which could not be funded from the medium-term loan.

The construction project was temporarily halted for three weeks in May due to substantial technical and administrative work being carried out.

It is assumed that management of Morskoy Inc. adopted the accounting policy of capitalizing borrowing costs.

The following amounts of debt were outstanding at the balance sheet date, 31 December 20x2:

	$
• Medium-term loan (see above)	800,000
• Bank overdraft	1,200,500
(The weighted average amount outstanding during the year was $750,000 and total interest charged by the bank amounted to $33,800 for the year)	
• A 10%, 7-year note dated 1 October 19x7 with simple interest payable annually at 31 December	9,000,000

The amount to be capitalized to the cost price of the warehouse in 20x2 can be calculated as follows:

Specific loan	**$**
$800,000 x 9% x 9/12	54,000
Interest earned on unused portion of loan available during the year:	
• 1 April to 30 June [(800,000 – 450,000) x 3/12 x 6%]	(5,250)
• 1 July to 31 October [(800,000 – 550,000) x 4/12 x 6%]	(5,000)
• 1 November to 30 November [(800,000 – 750,000) x 1/12 x 6%]	(250)
	43,500

CASE STUDY
CONTINUED

BORROWING COSTS

General pool of funds
Capitalization rate is 9.58% **(Calculation a)**

Paid on 31 January (200,000 x 11/12 x 9.58%)	17,563
Paid on 30 November (200,000 x 1/12 x 9.58%)	1,597
	19,160

TOTAL AMOUNT TO BE CAPITALIZED	62,660

NOTE: Although the activities had been interrupted by technical and administrative work during May 20x2, capitalization is not suspended for this period according to IAS 23.

CALCULATION

			$
a.	**Capitalization rate for pool of debt**		
	Total interest paid on these borrowings		
	• Bank overdraft		33,800
	• 7-year note (9,000,000 x 10%)		900,000
			933,800
	Weighted average total borrowings		
	• Bank overdraft		750,000
	• 7-year note		9,000,000
			9,750,000
	Capitalization rate	=	933,800 ÷ 9,750,000
		=	9.58% (rounded)

CHAPTER 20

RELATED PARTY DISCLOSURES (IAS 24)

20.1 PROBLEMS ADDRESSED

A related party relationship can have a significant influence on the financial position and operating results of the reporting entity. The objective of the IAS is to define related party relationships and transactions and to enhance disclosure thereof.

20.2 SCOPE OF THE STANDARD

The IAS should be applied when dealing with related parties and related party transactions. The requirements apply to the financial statements of **each** reporting related party.

20.3 ACCOUNTING TREATMENT

20.3.1 Parties are considered to be related if one party has the ability to control (or jointly control) the other party or exercise significant influence over the other party in making financing and operating decisions. Related party relationships **include**:

- Entities that directly control, are controlled by, or are under common control with the reporting entity (e.g., a group of companies).
- Associates.
- Jointly controlled entities.
- Individuals, including close family members, owning, directly or indirectly, interest in the voting power in the reporting entity that gives them significant influence.
- Key management personnel (including directors, officers, and close family members) responsible for planning, directing, and controlling the activities.
- Entities in which a substantial interest in the voting power is held, either directly or indirectly, by individuals (key personnel and close family members) or entities over which these people can exercise significant influence.

20.3.2 A related party transaction comprises a transfer of resources or obligations between related parties, regardless of whether or not a price is charged; this includes transactions concluded on an arms length basis. The following are examples of these transactions:

- Purchase or sale of goods.
- Purchase or sale of property or other assets.
- Rendering or receipt of services.
- Agency arrangements.
- Lease agreements.
- Transfer of research and development.
- License agreements.
- Finance, including loans and equity contributions.
- Guarantees and collaterals.
- Management contracts.

20.3.3 Related party relationships are a normal feature in commerce. Many entities carry on separate parts of their activities through subsidiaries, associates, joint ventures, etc. These parties sometimes enter into transactions through atypical business terms and prices.

20.3.4 Related parties have a degree of flexibility in the price setting process that is not present in transactions between related parties, for example:
- Comparable uncontrolled price method.
- Resale price method.
- Cost-plus method.

20.4   DISCLOSURE

20.4.1 The following are to be disclosed in the **notes** to the financial statements:
- Specify the related party relationships where **control** exists, irrespective of whether or not there have been transactions between the parties.
- If related party transactions occurred:
  - Nature of related party relationships.
  - Types of the transactions.
  - Elements of the transactions, being:
    - Volume (either as an amount or an appropriate proportion).
    - Amount or appropriate proportions of outstanding items.
    - Pricing policies.

20.4.2 **No disclosure** of transactions is required in:
- Consolidated financial statements in respect of intra-group transactions.
- Parent financial statements included with the consolidated financial statements.
- Financial statements of a wholly-owned subsidiary if its parent is in the same country and prepares group statements.
- Financial statements of state-controlled enterprises of transactions with similar enterprises.

---------------------------------- CASE STUDY ----------------------------------

RELATED PARTY DISCLOSURES

Habitat Inc. is a subsidiary in a group structure, which is indicated by the following diagram:

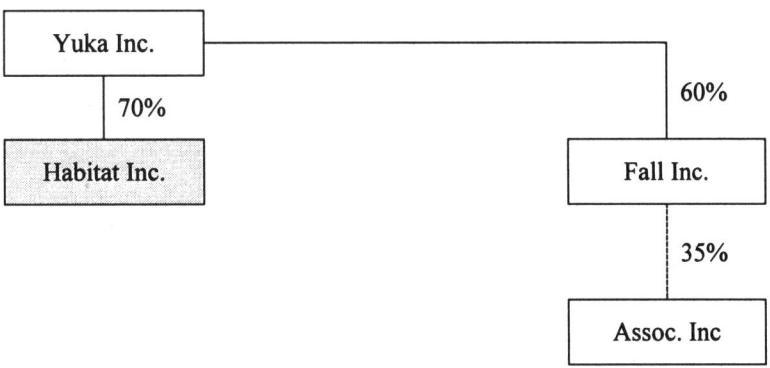

*Solid lines indicate **control** whereas dotted lines indicate the exercise of **significant influence**.*

During the year Habitat Inc. acquired plant and equipment from Assoc. Inc. at an amount of $23 million on which Assoc. Inc. earned a profit of $4 million.

Habitat Inc. and Assoc. Inc. are deemed to be related parties in terms of IAS 24. The full details of the transaction should therefore be disclosed in the financial statement of **both** entities as required by IAS 24, namely:
- Nature of the related party relationship.
- The nature of the transaction.
- Amount involved.
- Any amount still due by Habitat Inc. to Assoc. Inc.
- Pricing policy for determining the transaction amount.

Chapter 21

Accounting and Reporting by Retirement Benefit Plans (IAS 26)

The IAS prescribes the information that should be reported by each retirement benefit plan about its nature, financial resources, and performance.

The standard should be applied to the reports of retirement benefit plans that are directed to **all participants**, irrespective of whether a plan is:

- A separate fund or not.
- A defined contribution or a defined benefit plan.
- Managed by an insurance company.
- Sponsored by other parties than employees.
- A formal or informal agreement.

21.3.1   Retirement benefit plans could either be **defined contribution** or **defined benefit plans** (refer to chapter 15).

21.3.2   The involvement of actuaries with retirement benefit plans could be summarized as follows:
- **Defined contribution plans**: An employer's obligation is usually discharged by its contributions. An actuary's advice is therefore not normally required.
- **Defined benefit plans**: Periodic advice of an actuary is required to assess the financial condition of the plan, review the assumptions, and recommend future contribution levels. An employer is responsible for restoring the level of a benefit plan when deficits occur, in order to provide the agreed benefits to current and former employees.

DEFINED CONTRIBUTIONS PLANS

21.3.3   The following principles apply to the valuation of assets owned by the plan:
- Investments should be carried at fair value.
- If carried at other amounts, the fair value should be disclosed.

21.3.4   The **report of a defined contribution plan** should contain a statement of net assets available for benefits and a description of the funding policy.

DEFINED BENEFIT PLANS

21.3.5   Actuarial valuations are normally obtained every three years. The present value of the expected payments by a defined benefit plan may be calculated and reported using current salary levels **or** projected salary levels up to the time of retirement of participants.

21.3.6   The rules for the valuation of plan assets are similar to those for defined contribution plans.

21.3.7 The **report of a defined benefit plan** contains information that should be presented in **one** of the following formats:

- The report shows the net assets available for benefits, the actuarial present value of retirement benefits expected to become payable in the future, and the resulting excess or deficit. It also contains statements of changes in net assets available for benefits, and changes in the actuarial present value of promised retirement benefits. The report **may** include a separate actuary's report supporting the actuarial present value of promised retirement benefits.
- The same information on net assets are provided as above, but the actuarial present value is disclosed in a note. The report **may** also include a separate actuary's report as above.
- The report includes a statement of net assets available for benefits and a statement of changes in those assets with the actuarial present value contained in a **separate** actuarial report.

21.4   DISCLOSURE

Description of the plan

Information such as the names of the employers and the employee groups covered, number of participants receiving benefits, type of plan, and other details are required.

Policies

- Significant accounting policies.
- Description of the investment policies.
- Description of the funding policy.

Statement of net assets available for benefits

This statement shows the amount of assets available to pay retirement benefits that are expected to become payable in future.

- Assets at year-end, suitably classified.
- Basis of valuation of assets.
- When plan investments are held because an estimate of fair value is not possible, disclosure is made of the reason.
- Details of any single investment exceeding either 5% of net assets available for benefits or 5% of any class or type of security.
- Details of any investment in the employer.
- Liabilities other than the actuarial present value of promised retirement benefits.

Statement of changes in net assets available for benefits

- Investment income.
- Employer contributions.
- Employee contributions.
- Other income.
- Benefits paid or payable (analyzed per category of benefit).
- Administrative expenses.
- Other expenses.
- Taxes on income.
- Profits and losses on disposal of investments and changes in value of investments.
- Transfers from and to other plans.

Actuarial information (for benefit plans only):

- The actuarial present value of promised retirement benefits, based on the benefits promised under the terms of the plan, on service rendered to date, and on using either current salary levels or projected salary levels.
- Description of main actuarial assumptions.
- Method used to calculate the actuarial present value of promised retirement benefits.
- Date of most recent actuarial valuation.

CASE STUDY

ACCOUNTING AND REPORTING BY RETIREMENT BENEFIT PLANS

The report of a retirement benefit plan should *inter alia* contain a statement of changes in net assets available for benefits.

The following extract was taken from the **World Bank Group: Staff Retirement Plan – 1996 Annual Report**. It contains such statements which complies with the IAS 26 requirements in all material respects:

Statements of changes in net assets available for benefits

	Year ended December 31,	
	1996	1995
	$'000	$'000
Investment income		
Net appreciation in fair value of investments	809,008	694,402
Interest and dividends	301,391	233,163
Total investment income	1,110,399	927,565
Contributions		
Contributions by Bank/IFC/MIGA	101,337	113,217
Contributions by participants	55,651	55,341
Net receipts from pension plans of other international organizations on behalf of transferred participants	1,768	640
Total contributions	158,756	169,198
Total additions	1,269,155	1,096,763
Benefit payments		
Pensions	(110,034)	(95,299)
Commutation payments	(47,041)	(38,736)
Contributions, withdrawal benefits, and interest paid to former participants on withdrawal	(7,810)	(7,625)
Lump sum death benefits	(1,803)	(899)
Total deductions	(166,688)	(142,559)
Net increase	1,102,467	954,204
Net assets available for benefits		
Beginning of year	6,475,709	5,521,505
End of year	**7,578,176**	**6,475,709**

CHAPTER 22

CONSOLIDATED FINANCIAL STATEMENTS AND ACCOUNTING FOR INVESTMENTS IN SUBSIDIARIES (IAS 27)

22.1 PROBLEMS ADDRESSED

Users of the financial statements of a parent enterprise need information about the financial position, results of operations, and changes in financial position of the group as a whole. The IAS prescribes the following:

- Procedures for the preparation and presentation of consolidated financial statements.
- The accounting treatment of subsidiaries in a parent enterprise's separate financial statements.

22.2 SCOPE OF THE STANDARD

The IAS is applicable to a parent enterprise and the subsidiaries in the group that are controlled by the parent. Control is defined as the power to govern the financial and operating policies of an enterprise so as to obtain benefits from its activities. The existence of control is evidenced by *inter alia* one of the following:

- **Ownership**: parent owning (directly or indirectly) through subsidiaries more than 50% of the voting power.
- **Voting rights**: power over more than 50% of the voting rights by virtue of an agreement with other investors.
- **Policies**: power to govern the financial and operating policies of the enterprise under a statute or agreement.
- **Board of directors**: power to appoint or remove the majority of the members of the board of directors.
- **Voting rights of directors**: power to cast the majority of votes at meetings of the board.

*SIC–12 requires the consolidation of a **special purpose entity** when, in substance, it is controlled by a parent enterprise.*

22.3 ACCOUNTING TREATMENT

CONSOLIDATED FINANCIAL STATEMENTS

22.3.1 A parent should present consolidated financial statements as if the group were a single enterprise. A wholly owned subsidiary, or one that is virtually wholly owned, need not present consolidated financial statements.

22.3.2 A parent should consolidate all subsidiaries, foreign and domestic, except for the following, which are excluded:

- Subsidiaries acquired and held with a view to its subsequent disposal in the near future.
- Subsidiaries operating under severe long-term restrictions that significantly impair its ability to transfer funds.

Such subsidiaries are accounted for as investments in terms of IAS 39; see chapter 34.

22.3.3 The basic approach to preparing a set of consolidated financial statements is to combine the financial statements of the parent and its subsidiaries on a line-by-line basis by adding together like items of assets, liabilities, equity, income, and expenses. Other basic procedures include:

- The carrying amount of the parent's investment and its portion of equity of each subsidiary are eliminated in accordance with the procedures of IAS 22; see chapter 18.

- Minority interests in the net assets of consolidated subsidiaries are identified and presented in the consolidated balance sheet separately.
- Intragroup balances and intragroup transactions are eliminated.
- Unrealized profits/losses are eliminated.
- Minority interests in the profit/loss of subsidiaries for the period are identified and presented separately in the income statement. It is adjusted against the profit/loss of the group in order to arrive at the net profit/loss attributable to the owners of the parent.
- Taxes are treated in terms of IAS 12.
- Consolidated profits are adjusted for the subsidiary's cumulative preferred dividends, whether or not dividends have been declared.
- An investment should be accounted for in terms of IAS 39, from the date that it ceases to be a subsidiary and does not become an associate.
- The losses applicable to the minority interest may exceed its interest in the equity of the subsidiary. The excess is charged against the **majority** interest except to the extent that the minority has a binding obligation to, and is able to, make good on the losses.

22.3.4 Other consolidation procedures include the following:
- Uniform accounting policies should be used.
- When the reporting dates of the parent and subsidiaries differ, adjustments are made for significant transactions or events that occur between those dates. The difference should be no more than 3 months.

PARENT ENTERPRISE'S OWN FINANCIAL STATEMENTS

22.3.5 In a parent enterprise's separate financial statements, investments in subsidiaries that are included in the consolidated financial statements should be either:
- carried at cost,
- equity accounted in terms of IAS 28, **or**
- accounted for as available-for-sale financial assets in terms of IAS 39.

22.4 DISCLOSURE

22.4.1 CONSOLIDATED FINANCIAL STATEMENTS
- Listing of significant subsidiaries:
  - Names.
  - Country of incorporation/residence.
  - Proportion of ownership interest or proportion of voting power (if different).
- Reasons for not consolidating a subsidiary.
- Nature of the relationship when the parent does not own (directly/indirectly) more than 50% of the voting power.
- Name of an enterprise in which more than 50% of the voting power is owned (directly/indirectly), but which, because of the absence of control, is not a subsidiary.
- The effect of acquisition and disposal of subsidiaries on the financial position, and the results for the reporting period and on the comparative amounts.
- Where the parent is wholly owned, state:
  - Reasons for not preparing consolidated financial statements.
  - Bases on which subsidiaries are accounted in its own financial statements.
  - Name and registered office of its parent.
- If uniform accounting policies are not used:
  - The fact to be stated.
  - Proportions of items affected is shown.

22.4.2 PARENT'S OWN FINANCIAL STATEMENTS
- Method(s) used to account for subsidiaries.

CASE STUDY

CONSOLIDATED FINANCIAL STATEMENTS AND ACCOUNTING FOR INVESTMENTS IN SUBSIDIARIES

A.   The following amounts of profit after tax relate to the Alpha group of entities:

	$
Alpha Inc.	150,000
Beta Inc.	40,000
Charlie Inc.	25,000
Delta Inc.	60,000
Echo Inc.	80,000

- Alpha Inc. owns 75% of the voting power in Beta Inc. and 30% of the voting power n Charlie Inc.
- Beta Inc. also owns 30% of the voting power in Charlie Inc. and 25% of the voting power in Echo Inc.
- Charlie Inc. owns 40% of the voting power in Delta Inc.

ISSUES: What is the status of each entity in the group and how is the minority share in the group profit after tax calculated?

Beta Inc. and Charlie Inc. are both **subsidiaries** of Alpha Inc. which owns, directly or indirectly through a subsidiary more than 50% of the voting power in the entities.

Charlie Inc. and Echo Inc. are deemed to be **associates** of Beta Inc., while Delta Inc. is deemed to be an **associate** of Charlie Inc. unless it can be demonstrated that significant influence does not exist.

The minority interest in the group profit after tax is calculated as follows:

	$	$
Profit after tax of Charlie Inc.		
• Own	25,000	
• Equity accounted:		
▪ Delta Inc. (40% x 60,000)	24,000	
	49,000	
• Minority interest of 40%		19,600
Profit after tax of Beta Inc.		
• Own	40,000	
• Equity accounted:		
▪ Charlie Inc. (30% x 49,000)	14,700	
▪ Echo Inc. (25% x 8,000)	20,000	
	74,700	
• Minority interest of 25%		18,675
		38,275

CONSOLIDATED FINANCIAL STATEMENTS AND ACCOUNTING FOR INVESTMENTS IN SUBSIDIARIES

B.   A European parent company, with subsidiaries in various countries, follows the accounting policy of LIFO costing for all inventories in the group. It has recently acquired a controlling interest in a South African subsidiary that is not allowed to follow this policy due to local accounting pronouncements.

ISSUE: How is this aspect dealt with on consolidation?

IAS 27 requires consolidated financial statements to be prepared using uniform accounting principles, as far as it is practicable. However, it does not demand that an entity in the group changes its method of accounting to that which is adopted for the group.

One of the following options may be followed:

- Appropriate adjustments may be made to the financial statements of the SA subsidiary to convert the value of inventories to a LIFO-based value for purposes of preparing the consolidated financial statements.
- If it is not practicable to use a uniform accounting policy for inventories (e.g., from a cost-benefit point of view to do the conversion), the fact should be disclosed, together with the amount of inventory that is not based on the LIFO formula.

Chapter 23

Accounting for Investments in Associates (IAS 28)

23.1	PROBLEMS ADDRESSED

This IAS describes the alternative accounting treatments for associates. Its main objective is to provide users with information concerning the investors' interest in the earnings and in the underlying assets and liabilities of the investee.

23.2	SCOPE OF THE STANDARD

This IAS is applicable to each investment in an associate; an associate is an enterprise that the investor has significant influence in, but is neither a subsidiary nor a joint venture of the investor.

23.3	ACCOUNTING TREATMENT

23.3.1 **Significant influence** is the power to **participate** in financial and operating policy decisions of an investee, but not to control these policies. Existence of significant influence is evidenced by, *inter alia*:

- Holding (directly or indirectly) greater than or equal to 20% of voting power unless no significant influence is demonstrated.
- Representation on the governing body.
- Participation in policy making processes.
- Material transactions between parties.
- Interchange of managerial personnel.
- Provision of essential technical information.

23.3.2 The following methods could be used to account for investments in associates:

- **The equity method:** A method whereby the investment is initially recorded at cost and adjusted for the post acquisition change in the investor's share of net assets of the investee. The carrying amount is reduced for distributions received (e.g., dividends).
- **The cost method:** A method whereby the investment is recorded at cost. The income statement reflects income only to the extent that the investor receives distributions from accumulated net profits of the investee that arise subsequent to the date of acquisition. Distributions in excess of such profits reduce the carrying amount.

23.3.3 Associates are normally accounted for in the **consolidated financial statements** under the equity method. However, such investment is accounted for in accordance with IAS 39 when:

- the investment is acquired and held for disposal in the near future, **or**
- it operates under severe long-term restrictions.

23.3.4 In its **separate financial statements** the investor accounts for associates by either:

- carrying it at cost,
- using the equity method of accounting, **or**
- accounting for it as available-for-sale financial assets in terms of IAS 39.

23.3.5 Other accounting principles of the **equity method** are:
- Start equity accounting from the date that the investee meets the definition of an associate.
- Discontinue equity accounting when:
  - the investor ceases to have significant influence, but retains whole or part of the investment, **or**
  - the associate operates under severe long-term restrictions that significantly impair its ability to transfer funds.
- Many procedures for the equity method are similar to **consolidation procedures**, such as:
  - Eliminating unrealized profits/losses arising from transactions between the investor and the investee *(SIC–3)*.
  - Identifying the goodwill portion of the purchase price.
  - Amortization of goodwill.
  - Adjustments for depreciation of depreciable assets, based on their fair values.
  - Adjustments for the effect of cross holdings.
  - Using uniform accounting policies.
- The most recent financial statements of the associate are used for equity accounting.
- If reporting dates differ, make adjustments for significant events after the balance sheet date of the associate.
- The investor computes its share of profits or losses after adjusting for the cumulative preferred dividends, whether or not they have been declared.
- The investor recognizes losses of an associate until the investment is zero. Further losses are only provided for to the extent of guarantees given by the investor *(SIC–20)*.
- If there is an indication that an investment in an associate may be impaired, the enterprise applies IAS 36 (for each investment separately).

23.4   DISCLOSURE

Accounting policies
- Method used to account for:
  - Associates.
  - Goodwill and negative goodwill.
  - Amortization period for goodwill.

Income statement and notes
- Investor's share of:
  - Profits and losses for the period.
  - Extraordinary items.
  - Prior period items.

Balance sheet and notes
- Investment in associate(s) shown as a separate item on the face and classified as non-current.
- An appropriate list and description of significant associates, including:
  - Name.
  - Nature of the business.
  - Proportion of ownership interest or proportion of voting power (if different from the ownership interest).
- If the investor does not present consolidated financial statements and does not equity-account the investment, disclose what would have been the effect had the equity method been applied.
- If it is not practicable to calculate adjustments when associate(s) uses accounting policies other than those adopted by investor, the fact should be mentioned.
- The investor's share of the contingent liabilities and capital commitments of an associate for which it is contingently liable.

CASE STUDY

ACCOUNTING FOR INVESTMENTS IN ASSOCIATES

Dolo Inc. acquired a 40% interest in the ordinary shares of Nutro Inc. on the date of incorporation, 1 January 20x0, for an amount of $220,000. This enabled Dolo Inc. to exercise significant influence over Nutro Inc. On 31 December 20x3 the shareholders' equity of Nutro Inc. was as follows:

		$
•	Ordinary issued share capital	550,000
•	Reserves	180,000
•	Accumulated profit	650,000
		1,380,000

The following abstracts were taken from the financial statements of Nutro Inc. for the year ending 31 December 20x4:

	$
Income statement	
Profit after tax	228,000
Extraordinary item	(12,000)
Net profit for the period	216,000
Statement of changes in equity	
Accumulated profits at beginning of the year	650,000
Net profit for the period	216,000
Dividends paid	(80,000)
Accumulated profits at end of the year	786,000

During November 20x4, Dolo Inc. sold inventories to Nutro Inc. for the first time. The total sales amounted to $50,000 and Dolo Inc. earned a profit of $10,000 on the transaction. None of the inventories had been sold by Nutro Inc. by 31 December. The income tax rate is 30%.

The application of the equity method would result in the carrying amount of the investment in Nutro Inc. being reflected as follows:

	$
Original cost	220,000
Post-acquisition profits accounted for at beginning of the year	
[40% x (180,000 + 650,000)]	332,000
Carrying amount on 1 January 20x4	552,000
Attributable portion of net profit for the period **(Calculation a)**	83,600
Dividends received (40% x 80,000)	(32,000)
	603,600

CASE STUDY

CONTINUED

ACCOUNTING FOR INVESTMENTS IN ASSOCIATES

CALCULATION

		$
a.	**Attributable portion of net profit**	86,400
	Net profit (40% x 216,000)	(2,800)
	After-tax effect of unrealized profit [40% x (70% x 10,000)]	83,600

SIC–3 requires that unrealized gains and losses resulting from transactions with associates, under IAS 28.16, be eliminated proportionately

---

CHAPTER 24

FINANCIAL REPORTING IN HYPERINFLATIONARY ECONOMIES (IAS 29)

24.1 PROBLEMS ADDRESSED

In a hyperinflationary economy, reporting of operating results and financial position without **restatement** is not useful. Money loses purchasing power at such a rate that comparison of amounts from transactions and other events that have occurred, even within the same accounting period, is misleading. This IAS requires that the financial statements of an enterprise operating in a hyperinflationary economy be restated.

24.2 SCOPE OF THE STANDARD

The IAS should be applied by enterprises that report in hyperinflationary economies. Characteristics of a hyperinflationary economy include:
- The general population prefers to keep its wealth in non-monetary assets or in a relatively stable foreign currency.
- Prices are normally quoted in a stable foreign currency.
- Credit transactions take place at prices that compensate for the expected loss of purchasing power.
- Interest, wages, and prices are linked to price indices.
- The cumulative inflation rate over three years is approaching or is greater than 100% (i.e. an average of more than 26% p.a.).

24.3 ACCOUNTING TREATMENT

24.3.1 The financial statements of an enterprise that reports in the currency of a hyperinflationary economy should be restated in the measuring unit current at the balance sheet date; i.e.,the enterprise should adjust the amounts in the financial statements as if they occurred in the reporting currency **on the balance sheet date** only.

24.3.2 The restated financial statements **replace** the normal financial statements and do not serve as a supplement thereto. Separate presentation of the normal financial statements is discouraged.

RESTATEMENT OF HISTORICAL COST FINANCIAL STATEMENTS

24.3.3 **General rules** of restatement include the following:
- Comparatives are restated in the measuring unit at the balance sheet date. This implies that even prior year cash amounts are adjusted by the current-year's inflation index.
- A reliable general price index should be used that reflects changes in general purchasing power. Where not available, a relatively stable foreign currency is used.
- Restatement starts from the beginning of the financial year in which hyperinflation is identified.
- When hyperinflation ceases, restatement is discontinued.

24.3.4 Rules applicable to the restatement of the **balance sheet** are:
- Monetary items are not restated.

- Index-linked assets and liabilities are restated in accordance with the agreement.
- Non-monetary items are restated in terms of the current measuring unit by applying the changes in the index or currency unit to the carrying values since date of acquisition (or the first period of restatement) or fair values on dates of valuation.
- Non-monetary assets are not restated if they are shown at net realizable value, fair value, or recoverable amount at balance sheet date.
- At the beginning of the first period in which the principles of IAS 29 are applied, components of owners' equity, except accumulated profits and any revaluation surplus, are restated from the dates the components were contributed.
- At the end of the first period and subsequently, all components of owners' equity are restated from the date of contribution.
- The movements in owners' equity are included in equity.

24.3.5   All items in the **income statement** are restated by applying the change in the reliable general price index from the dates when the items were initially recorded.

24.3.6   A **gain or loss on the net monetary position** is included in net income. This amount may be estimated by applying the change in the general price index to the weighted average of net monetary assets/liabilities.

RESTATEMENT OF CURRENT COST FINANCIAL STATEMENTS

24.3.7   Rules applicable to the restatement of the **balance sheet** are:
- Items shown at current cost are not restated.
- Other items are restated in terms of the rules above.

24.3.8   All amounts included in the **income statement** are restated into the measuring unit at balance sheet date by applying the general price index.

24.3.9   If a **gain or loss on the net monetary position** is calculated in terms of IAS 15, such an adjustment forms part of the gain or loss on the net monetary position calculated in terms of IAS 29.

24.3.10 All cash flows are expressed in terms of the measuring unit at **balance sheet date**.

24.3.11 When a foreign subsidiary, associate, or joint venture of a parent company reports in a hyperinflationary economy, the financial statements of such entities should first be **restated** in accordance with IAS 29 and then translated at **closing rate** as if they are foreign entities per IAS 21.

24.4   DISCLOSURE

The following aspects should be disclosed:
- The fact of restatement.
- The fact that comparatives are restated.
- Whether the financial statements are based on the historical cost approach or the current cost approach.
- The identity and the level of the price index or stable currency at balance sheet date.
- The movement in price index or stable currency during the current and previous financial years.

CASE STUDY

FINANCIAL REPORTING IN HYPERINFLATIONARY ECONOMIES

Darbrow Inc. was incorporated on 1 January of 20x2 with an equity capital of $40 million. The balance sheets of the entity at the beginning and end of the first financial year were as follows:

	Beginning $'000	End $'000
Assets		
Property, plant and equipment	60,000	50,000
Inventory	30,000	40,000
Receivables	50,000	60,000
	140,000	150,000
Equity and liabilities		
Share capital	40,000	40,000
Accumulated profit	–	10,000
Borrowings	100,000	100,000
	140,000	150,000

The income statement for the first year reflected the following amounts:

	$'000
Revenue	800,000
Operating expenses	(750,000)
Depreciation of plant and equipment	(10,000)
Operating profit	40,000
Interest paid	(20,000)
Profit before tax	20,000
Income tax expense	(10,000)
Profit after tax	10,000

Additional information

1. The rate of inflation was 120% for the year.
2. The inventory represents two months' purchases, and all income statement items accrued evenly during the year.

CASE STUDY

CONTINUED

FINANCIAL REPORTING IN HYPERINFLATIONARY ECONOMIES

The financial statements may be restated to the measuring unit at balance sheet date using a **reliable price index** as follows:

BALANCE SHEET

	Recorded $'000	Restated $'000	Calculations
Assets			
Property, plant and equipment	50,000	110,000	2.20/1.00
Inventory **(Calculation a)**	40,000	41,905	2.20/2.10
Receivables	60,000	60,000	
	150,000	211,905	
Equity and liabilities			
Share capital	40,000	88,000	2.20/1.00
Accumulated profits	10,000	23,905	balancing
Borrowings	100,000	100,000	
	150,000	211,905	

INCOME STATEMENT

	$'000	$'000	
Revenue **(Calculation b)**	800,000	1,100,000	2.20/1.60
Operating expenses	(750,000)	(1,031,250)	2.20/1.60
Depreciation **(Calculation c)**	(10,000)	(22,000)	2.20/1.00
Interest paid	(20,000)	(27,500)	2.20/1.60
Income tax expense	(10,000)	(13,750)	2.20/1.60
Net profit before restatement gain	10,000	5,500	
Gain arising from			balancing
inflationary adjustment		18,405	figure
Net profit after restatement gain		23,905	

CALCULATIONS

a.   **Index for inventory**
     Inventory purchased on average at 30 November
     Index at that date = $1.00 + (1.20 \times 11/12) = 2.10$

b.   **Index for income and expenses**
     Average for the year = $1.00 + (1.20 \div 2) = 1.60$

c.   **Index for depreciation**
     Linked to the index of property, plant and equipment = 1.00

CHAPTER 25

DISCLOSURES IN THE FINANCIAL STATEMENTS OF BANKS AND SIMILAR FINANCIAL INSTITUTIONS (IAS 30)

It should be emphasized that all IASs are applicable to banks, particularly IAS 32 and 39. As IAS 30 was written before IAS 32 and 39, some of the requirements will overlap, and any other disclosure requirements per IAS 30 (mostly related to the risk-based classification of assets and liabilities) should be regarded as supplementary (see Appendix III at the back of the book).

25.1   PROBLEMS ADDRESSED

The users of bank financial statements need a better understanding of the special operations of a bank, and in particular its **solvency, liquidity** and also the **relative degree of risk** that attaches to the different areas of its business. The objective of this IAS is to:

- Describe the **reporting requirements** of a bank.
- Encourage management to provide a commentary on the financial statements that describes the way it manages and controls its **liquidity** and **solvency**, as well as the **full spectrum of risks** associated with the operations of the bank.

Banks are exposed to various operational and financial risks. Although some of the banking risks may be reflected in the financial statements, users obtain a better understanding if management provides a commentary that describes the way it **manages** and **controls** these risks. *Although management commentary is only recommended by IAS 30, this is now a required disclosure in IAS 32, paragraph 43A.*

25.2   SCOPE OF THE STANDARD

This standard is applicable to all banks. Banks are defined as those financial institutions that, *inter alia*, take deposits and borrow from the general public with the objective of lending and investing within the scope of banking or similar legislation.

25.3   ACCOUNTING TREATMENT

25.3.1   The standard does not establish specific recognition and measurement criteria for banks, because **the same exact accounting principles** (as set out in the other standards) should be applied by banks for the recording of transactions and events. This IAS therefore deals with **disclosures** only.

25.3.2   Although a bank is subject to supervision and provides the regulatory authorities with information, that information is not always available to all users. Therefore, disclosure in the financial statements needs to be sufficiently comprehensive to meet the needs of users (within the reasonable constraints).

25.4   DISCLOSURE

25.4.1   The **accounting policy notes** should disclose the bases on which financial statements are prepared, including:

- Recognition of principal types of income.
- Valuation of investment and dealing securities.

99

- Distinction between those transactions and other events that result in the recognition of assets and liabilities (balance sheet items) and those only giving rise to contingencies and commitments (off-balance sheet items).
- Determination of losses on loans and advances and for writing off uncollectable loans and advances.
- Determination of charges for general banking risks and the accounting treatment of such charges.

25.4.2 The **income statement** should group income and expenses by nature and disclose the amounts of the principal types of income and expenses. In addition to the requirements of other IASs, the income statement or the notes should include:
- Interest and similar income.
- Interest expense and similar charges.
- Dividend income.
- Fee and commission income.
- Fee and commission expense.
- Gains less losses arising from dealing securities.
- Gains less losses arising from investment securities.
- Gains less losses arising from dealing in foreign currencies.
- Other operating income.
- Losses on loans and advances.
- General administrative expenses.
- Other operating expenses.

Income and expense items should not be offset except for those relating to hedges and to assets and liabilities that have been offset in the balance sheet.

The following gains and losses are normally reported on a net basis:
- Disposals and changes in the carrying amount of dealing securities.
- Disposals of investment securities.
- Dealing in foreign currencies.

Management should provide a **commentary** about average interest rates, average interest-earning assets, and average interest-bearing liabilities for the period.

25.4.3 The balance sheet should group assets and liabilities by nature and list them in an order that reflects their relative liquidity. In addition to the requirements of other IASs, the balance sheet or the notes should include:
- **Assets**
  - Cash and balances with the central bank.
  - Treasury bills and other bills eligible for rediscounting with the central bank.
  - Government and other securities held for dealing purposes.
  - Placements with, and loans and advances to, other banks.
  - Other money market placements.
  - Loans and advances to customers.
  - Investment securities.

- **Liabilities**
  - Deposits from other banks.
  - Other money market deposits.
  - Amounts owed to other depositors.
  - Certificates of deposit.
  - Promissory notes and other liabilities evidenced by paper.
  - Other borrowed funds.

Assets and liabilities may be offset only if:
- a legal right to set-off exists, and
- there is an expectation of realizing an asset or settling a liability on a net basis.

Disclose the market values of dealing securities and marketable investment securities if they differ from the carrying amounts.

25.4.4 Disclose the following **contingencies and commitments** required by IAS 37 as well as **off-balance sheet** items:
- Nature and amount of commitments to **extend credit that are irrevocable**.
- Nature and amount of contingent liabilities and commitments arising from **off-balance sheet items** such as:
  - Direct credit substitutes, including general guarantees of indebtedness, bank acceptance guarantees, and standby letters of credit serving as financial guarantees for loans and securities.
  - Certain transaction-related contingent liabilities, including performance bonds, bid bonds, warranties and standby letters of credit related to particular transactions.
  - Short-term, self-liquidating, trade-related contingent liabilities arising from the movement of goods, such as documentary credits where the underlying shipment is used as security.
  - Sale and repurchase agreements not recognized in the balance sheet.
  - Interest and foreign exchange rate related items, including swaps, options, and futures.
  - Other commitments, note insurance facilities, and revolving underwriting facilities.

25.4.5 Disclose an analysis of **assets and liabilities into relevant maturity groupings** based on the remaining period at the balance sheet date to the contractual maturity date. Examples of periods used include:
- Up to 1 month.
- From 1 month to 3 months.
- From 3 months to 1 year.
- From 1 year to 5 years.
- Five years and over.

Maturities could be expressed in terms of the remaining period to the repayment date, original period to the repayment date, or remaining period to the next date at which interest rates may be changed.

Management should provide, in its **commentary**, information about the effective periods and about the way it manages and controls the risks and exposures associated with different maturity and interest rate profiles.

25.4.6 Disclose any **significant concentrations of the bank's assets, liabilities, and off-balance sheet items** in terms of geographical areas, customer or industry groups, or other concentrations of risk. A bank should also disclose the amount of significant net foreign currency exposures.

25.4.7 A bank should disclose the following information regarding **losses on loans and advances:**
- Details of movements in the provision for losses on loans and advances during the period, disclosing separately:
    - Amount recognized as provision for current period.
    - Amount written off for uncollectables.
    - Amount credited for recovered amounts.
- Aggregate amount of the provision for losses on loans and advances at balance sheet date.
- Aggregate amount for loans and advances on which interest is not being accrued, and the basis used to determine the carrying amount.

25.4.8 **Amounts set aside for general banking risks** (including future losses and other unforeseeable risks or contingencies in addition to those for which accrual must be made in accordance with IAS 37) should be separately disclosed as appropriations of accumulated profits. Any reductions of such amounts are credited directly to accumulated profits.

25.4.9 Disclose the aggregate amount of secured liabilities and the nature and carrying amount of the **assets pledged as security.**

25.4.10 If the bank is engaged in significant **trust activities**, the fact and an indication of the extent of those activities should be disclosed.

25.4.11 Comply with the requirements of IAS 24. The following elements would normally be disclosed in respect of **related party transactions**:
- Lending policy of the bank.
- Amount included in or the proportion of:
    - Loans and advances, deposits and acceptances, and promissory notes.
    - The principal types of income, interest expense, and commissions paid.
    - The expense recognized in the period for losses on loans and advances and the amount of the provision at the balance sheet date.
    - Irrevocable commitments and contingencies, and commitments arising from off-balance sheet items.

Appendix III to this book contains a table that summarizes and combines the disclosure requirements of IAS 1, 30, 32, and 39 **by risk category** for presentation in the financial statements of banks and similar institutions.

───────────────────── CASE STUDY ─────────────────────

DISCLOSURES IN THE FINANCIAL STATEMENTS OF BANKS AND SIMILAR FINANCIAL INSTITUTIONS

The following abstracts from a bank's annual financial statements refer to 'Advances', which are shown as separately disclosed assets on the face of the balance sheet:

ACCOUNTING POLICIES

1.   Doubtful advances

Advances are stated net of specific and general provisions. Specific provisions are made against identified doubtful advances. General provisions are maintained to cover potential losses which, although not specifically identified, may be present in any portfolio of advances. Accrual of interest on advances is suspended when the recoverability of the advance becomes uncertain.

Advances are written off once the probability of recovering any significant amounts becomes remote. Repossessed assets, including properties in possession, are stated at the lower of cost and net realizable value.

NOTES TO THE FINANCIAL STATEMENTS

		$m
2.	**Advances**	
	Overdrafts and credit cards	16,000
	Foreign currency loans	5,000
	Installment finance	22,000
	Mortgages	58,000
	Overnight finance	2,000
	Project finance	3,000
	Other	10,000
		116,000

Provisions for bad and doubtful advances (refer to note 4)		
• Specific provisions	5,000	
• General provisions	1,800	(6,800)
		109,200

2.1 Sectoral analysis	
Agriculture	3,000
Construction and property	2,000
Consumer	77,000
Finance	9,000
Manufacturing	7,000
Services	7,000
Transport	2,000
Wholesale	4,000
Other	5,000
	116,000

CASE STUDY
CONTINUED

DISCLOSURES IN THE FINANCIAL STATEMENTS OF BANKS AND SIMILAR FINANCIAL INSTITUTIONS

2.2 Maturity analysis

Within 1 year	33,000
From 1 year to 5 years	28,000
More than 5 years	55,000
	116,000

2.3 Geographical analysis

Central Asia	114,000
Other Asian countries	100
Europe	700
Africa	800
Americas	400
	116,000

The maturity analysis is based on the remaining period from year-end to contractual maturity

3.   Non-performing advances

	Gross balance $m	Non-performance balance $m	Security $m	Provision raised $m
Overdrafts and credit cards	16,000	2,000	1,300	1,000
Installment finance	22,000	1,000	900	500
Mortgages	58,000	5,000	6,700	2,500
Other	20,000	2,000	1,200	1,000
	116,000	10,000	10,100	5,000

4.   Provisions for bad and doubtful advances

	$m
Balance	
Balance at beginning of year	5,600
Amounts written off during year	(1,100)
	4,500
Provisions raised during year	2,300
Balance at end of year	6,800
Comprising:	
• Specific provisions	5,000
• General provisions	1,800
	6800
Charge in income statement	
Provision raised in current year	2,300
Recoveries of advances previously written off	(400)
	1,900

---- CASE STUDY ----
CONTINUED

DISCLOSURES IN THE FINANCIAL STATEMENTS OF BANKS AND SIMILAR FINANCIAL INSTITUTIONS

The usefulness of the disclosures above are evaluated as follows.

a.   **IAS 30, par 30: Analysis of assets into relevant maturity grouping based on time (Note 2.2).**

The maturities of assets and liabilities and the ability to replace, at an acceptable cost, liabilities as they mature, are important factors in assessing the liquidity of a bank and its exposure to changes in interest rates and exchange rates.

b.   **IAS 30, par. 40: Significant concentrations of assets in terms of geographical areas and customer/industry groups (Notes 2.1 & 2.3).**

This information is a useful indication of the potential risks inherent in the realization of the assets and the funds available to the bank.

c.   **IAS 30, par. 43(a): Accounting policy for the recognition and write-off of uncollectable loans and advances (Note 1).**

It assists the users in understanding the way in which transactions and events are reflected in the financial statements.

d.   **IAS 30, par. 43(b): Details of the movements in the provision for losses on loans and advances during the period; separately disclosing the amount recognized as an expense in the period, the amount charged in the period for loans and advances written off; and the amount credited in the period for loans and advances previously written off that have been recovered (Note 4).**

Users of the financial statements of a bank need to know the impact that losses on loans and advances have had on the financial position and performance of the bank; this helps them judge the effectiveness with which the bank has employed its resources.

e.   **IAS 30, par 43(c): The aggregate amount of the provisions for losses on loans and advances at the balance sheet date (Note 4).**

The amount of potential losses for future bad debts is reflected in the balance sheet.

f.   **IAS 30, par 43(d): The aggregate amount included in the balance sheet for loans and advances on which interest is not being accrued and the basis used to determine the carrying amount of such loans and advances (Notes 1 & 3).**

The impact that the non-accrual of interest has on the income statement is reflected.

CHAPTER 26

FINANCIAL REPORTING OF INTERESTS IN JOINT VENTURES (IAS 31)

26.1 PROBLEMS ADDRESSED

The alternative accounting treatments for joint ventures are described. The main objective is to provide users with information concerning the investing owners' (venturers) interest in the earnings and the underlying net assets of the joint venture.

26.2 SCOPE OF THE STANDARD

This IAS applies to interests in joint ventures and the reporting of their assets, liabilities, income, and expenses, regardless of their structures or forms (**substance over form**). A joint venture is a contractual arrangement whereby two or more parties undertake an economic activity that is subject to joint control.

26.3 ACCOUNTING TREATMENT

26.3.1 The following are characteristics of all joint ventures:
- Two or more venturers are bound by a contractual arrangement.
- This arrangement establishes joint control; i.e., the contractually agreed sharing of control over a joint venture such that not one of the parties can exercise unilateral control.

26.3.2 The existence of a **contractual arrangement** distinguishes joint ventures from associates. It is usually in writing and deals with such matters as:
- Activity, duration, and reporting.
- Appointment of a board of directors or equivalent body and voting rights.
- Capital contributions by venturers.
- Sharing by the venturers of the output, income, expenses, or results of the joint venture.

26.3.3 Joint ventures take many different forms and structures, namely **jointly controlled operations, assets, and entities**.

26.3.4 **Jointly controlled operations** involve the use of resources of the venturers rather than establishing separate structures. An example is when two or more parties combine resources and efforts to manufacture, market, and jointly sell a product. In respect of its interests in jointly controlled operations, a venturer should recognize in its **own** and **consolidated financial statements**:
- The assets that it controls.
- The liabilities that it incurs.
- The expenses that it incurs.
- Its share of the income that it earns.

26.3.5 **Jointly controlled assets**: Some joint ventures involve the joint control and ownership of one or more assets acquired for and dedicated to the purpose of the joint venture (e.g., factories sharing the same railway line). The establishment of a separate enterprise is unnecessary. A venturer should recognize in its **own** and **consolidated financial statements**:

- Its share of the assets.
- Any liabilities that it has incurred.
- Its share of any liabilities incurred jointly with the other venturers in relation to the joint venture.
- Any income it receives from the joint venture.
- Its share of any expenses incurred by the joint venture.
- Any expenses that it has incurred in respect of its interest in the joint venture.

26.3.6   Jointly controlled entities: Such a joint venture is conducted through **a separate enterprise** in which each venturer owns an interest. An example is when two enterprises combine their activities in a particular line of business by transferring assets and liabilities into a joint venture. A venturer reports its interest in a jointly controlled entity by choosing one of the following methods:

- **Benchmark**: Proportionate consolidation, whereby a venturer's share of each of the assets, liabilities, income, expenses, and cash flows of a jointly controlled entity is combined with similar items of the venturer or reported separately. The following principles apply:
  - Two formats may be used, namely:
    - combining items line by line, **or**
    - separate line items.
  - The interests in the joint ventures are included in the consolidated financial statements of the venturer, even if it has no subsidiaries.
  - Commence proportionate consolidation when the venturer acquires joint control.
  - Cease proportionate consolidation when the venturer loses joint control.
  - Many procedures for proportionate consolidation are similar to **consolidation procedures**, described in IAS 27.
  - Assets and liabilities may be offset only if:
    - a legal right to set-off exists, and
    - there is an expectation of realizing an asset or settling a liability on a net basis.
- **Alternative**: The equity method is an allowed alternative but not recommended. The method should be discontinued when joint control or significant influence is lost by the venturer.

The following **exceptions** to both treatments apply:

- Account for a joint venture as an investment in accordance with IAS 39, if:
  - Acquired and held with a view to subsequent disposal in the near future.
  - The joint venture operates under severe long-term restrictions that significantly impair its ability to transfer funds to the venturer.
- When the joint venture becomes a subsidiary, it is accounted for in terms of IAS 27.

26.3.7   The following **general accounting considerations** apply:

- Transactions between a venturer and a joint venture are treated as follows:
  - Eliminate the venturer's share of unrealized profits on sales or contribution of assets to a joint venture.
  - Eliminate full unrealized loss on sale or contribution of assets to a joint venture.
  - Eliminate the venturer's share of profits or losses on sales of assets by a joint venture to the venturer.

    SIC–13 addresses the accounting implications of non-monetary contributions by venturers.
- An investor in a joint venture, which does not have joint control, should report its interest in a joint venture in the **consolidated** financial statements in terms of IAS 39 or, if it has

significant influence, in terms of IAS 28. In its **separate** financial statements the investment may also be reported at cost.

- Operators or managers of a joint venture should account for any fees as revenue in terms of IAS 18.

26.4   DISCLOSURE

The following should be disclosed:

- Amount of the following contingent liabilities (IAS 37) to be shown **separately** from others:
  - Incurred jointly with other venturers.
  - Share of a joint venture's contingent liabilities.
  - Contingencies for liabilities of other venturers.
- Amount of the following commitments:
  - Incurred jointly with other venturers.
  - Share of a joint venture's commitments.
- Listing of significant joint ventures:
  - Names.
  - A description of the interests in all joint ventures.
  - The proportion of ownership.
- A venturer that uses the line-by-line reporting format or the equity method, should disclose aggregate amounts of each of the current assets, long-term assets, current liabilities, long-term liabilities, income, and expenses related to the joint ventures.
- A venturer not issuing consolidated financial statements (because it has no subsidiaries) should still disclose the above information.

CASE STUDY

FINANCIAL REPORTING OF INTERESTS IN JOINT VENTURES

Techno Inc. was incorporated after three independent engineering corporations decided to pool their knowledge to implement and market new technology. The three corporations acquired the following interests in the equity capital of Techno Inc. on the date of its incorporation:

- Electro Inc.   30%
- Mechan Inc.   40%
- Civil Inc.   30%

The following information was taken from the financial statements of Techno Inc. as well as one of the owners, Mechan Inc.

ABRIDGED INCOME STATEMENT FOR THE YEAR ENDING 30 JUNE 20x1

	Mechan Inc.	Techno Inc.
	$'000	$'000
Revenue	3,100	980
Cost of Sales	(1,800)	(610)
Gross profit	1,300	370
Other operating income	150	–
Operating costs	(850)	(170)
Profit before tax	600	200
Income tax expense	(250)	(90)
Net profit for the period	350	110

Mechan Inc. sold inventories with an invoice value of $600,000 to Techno Inc. during the year. Included in Techno Inc.'s inventories at 30 June 20x1 is an amount of $240,000, which is inventory purchased from Mechan Inc. at a profit mark-up of 20%. The income tax rate is 30%.

Techno Inc. paid an administration fee of $120,000 to Mechan Inc. during the year. This amount is included under "Other operating income."

In order to combine the results of Techno Inc. with those of Mechan Inc. the following issues would need to be resolved:
- Is Techno Inc. an associate or joint venture for financial reporting purposes?
- Which is the appropriate method for consolidating the results?
- How are the above transactions between the corporations to be recorded and presented for financial reporting purposes in the consolidated income statement?

First issue: The existence of a **contractual agreement**, whereby the parties involved undertake an economic activity subject to joint control, distinguishes a joint venture from an associate. No one of the ventures should be able to exercise unilateral control. However, in the event that no contractual agreement exists, the investment would be regarded as being an associate because the investor holds more than 20% of the voting power and is therefore presumed to have significant influence over the investee.

Second issue: If Techno Inc. is regarded as a joint venture, the proportionate consolidation method would be used. The equity method is also permitted as an allowed alternative treatment. However, if Techno Inc. is regarded as an associate, the equity method would be used.

CASE STUDY
CONTINUED

FINANCIAL REPORTING OF INTERESTS IN JOINT VENTURES

Third issue: It is assumed that Techno Inc. is a joint venture for purposes of this illustration.

CONSOLIDATED INCOME STATEMENT FOR THE YEAR ENDING 30 JUNE 20x1

	$'000
Revenue **(Calculation a)**	3,252
Cost of sales **(Calculation b)**	(1,820)
Gross profit	1432
Other operating income **(Calculation c)**	102
Operating costs **(Calculation d)**	(870)
Profit before tax	664
Income tax expense **(Calculation e)**	(281)
Net profit for the period	383

REMARKS

- The proportionate consolidation method is applied by adding 40% of the income statement items of Techno Inc. to those of Mechan Inc.
- The transactions between the corporations are then dealt with by recording the following consolidation journal entries:

	Dr $'000	Cr $'000
Sales (40% x 600)	240	
Cost of sales		240
(Eliminating intra-group sales)		
Cost of sales (40% x 20/120 x 240)	16	
Inventories		16
(Eliminating unrealized profit in inventory)		
Deferred taxation (B/S) (30% x 16)	4.8	
Income tax expense (I/S)		4.8
(Taxation effect on elimination of unrealized profit)		

- The administration fee is eliminated by reducing other operating income with Mechan Inc.'s portion of the total fee, namely $48,000, and reducing operating expenses accordingly. The net effect on the consolidated profit is nil.

─────── CASE STUDY ───────
CONTINUED

FINANCIAL REPORTING OF INTERESTS IN JOINT VENTURES

CALCULATIONS

		$'000

a. Sales

Mechan	3,100
Intra-group sales (40% x 600)	(240)
Techno (40% x 980)	392
	3,252

b. Cost of sales

Mechan	1,800
Intra-group sales	(240)
Unrealized profit (40% x 20/120 x 240)	16
Techno (40% x 610)	244
	1,820

c. Other operating income

Mechan	150
Intra-group fee (40% x 120)	(48)
	102

d. Operating costs

Mechan	850
Techno (40% x 170)	68
Intra-group fee (40% x 120)	(48)
	870

e. Income tax expense

Mechan	250
Unrealized profit (30% x 16 rounded-up)	(5)
Techno (40% x 90)	36
	281

CHAPTER 27

FINANCIAL INSTRUMENTS: DISCLOSURE AND PRESENTATION (IAS 32)

IAS 32 and 39 were issued as separate standards but are applied in practice as a unit because they deal with exactly the same accounting phenomenon. IAS 39, which deals with the Recognition and Measurement issues of financial instruments, also contains some supplementary disclosures to those required by IAS 32. These requirements are listed in this chapter in order to provide a comprehensive list of all the Disclosure and Presentation aspects related to financial instruments.

27.1 PROBLEMS ADDRESSED

Users need information that will enhance their understanding of the significance of on- and off-balance sheet financial instruments regarding an enterprise's financial position, performance and cash flows, and the assessment of the amounts, timing, and certainty of future cash flows associated with those instruments. This IAS:

- Prescribes requirements for the **presentation** of on-balance sheet financial instruments.
- Identifies information that should be **disclosed** about both on-balance sheet (recognized) and off-balance sheet (unrecognized) financial instruments.

27.2 SCOPE OF THE STANDARD

The IAS deals with **all types of financial instruments**, both recognized and unrecognized. A **financial instrument** is any contract that gives rise to both a financial asset of one enterprise and a financial liability or equity instrument of another.

27.3 ACCOUNTING TREATMENT

27.3.1 A **financial asset** is any asset that is:

- cash (e.g., deposit at a bank),
- a contractual right to receive cash or a financial asset (e.g., a debtor and derivative instrument),
- a contractual right to exchange financial instruments under potentially favorable conditions, **or**
- an equity instrument of another enterprise (e.g., investment in shares).

Physical assets (e.g., inventories and patents) are not financial assets, as they do not give rise to a present right to receive cash or other financial assets.

27.3.2 A **financial liability** is a contractual obligation to:

- deliver any financial asset (e.g., a creditor and derivative instrument), **or**
- exchange financial instruments under potentially unfavorable conditions.

Liabilities imposed by statutory requirements (e.g., income taxes) are not financial liabilities because they are not contractual.

27.3.3 An **equity instrument** is any contract that evidences a residual interest in the assets of an enterprise after deducting all of its liabilities. An obligation to issue an equity instrument is not a financial liability because it results in an increase in equity and cannot result in a loss to the enterprise.

27.3.4 The issuer of a financial instrument classifies it or components thereof as a liability or as equity in accordance with the:
- Substance of the contractual arrangement on initial recognition.
- Definitions above.

Substance over form governs the classification (e.g., a redeemable preferred share creates an obligation, which makes it a financial liability rather than equity).

27.3.5 The issuer of a **compound financial instrument** that contains **both** a liability and equity element (e.g., convertible bonds), should classify the instrument's component parts separately:
- Total amount – liability portion = equity portion.
- Equity valuation + liability valuation = total value. Assign carrying amount *pro rata* to the values so established.

Once so classified, the classification is not changed even if economic circumstances change. No gain or loss arises from recognizing and presenting the parts separately.

27.3.6 **Interest, dividends, losses, and gains** relating to a financial liability should be reported in the income statement as expense or income. Distributions to holders of an equity instrument should be debited **directly** to equity. The classification of the financial instrument determines the accounting treatment of the items mentioned above:
- Dividends on shares classified as liabilities would thus be classified as expense in the same way as interest payments on a loan. Furthermore, such dividends would have to be accrued over time.
- Gains and losses (presumably premiums and discounts) on redemption or refinancing of instruments classified as liabilities are reported in the **income statement**, while gains and losses on instruments classified as **equity** of the issuer are reported as movements in equity.

27.3.7 A financial asset and a financial liability should be **offset** only when:
- a legal enforceable right to set-off exists, and
- there is an intention either to settle on a net basis, or to realize the asset and settle the liability simultaneously.

27.4 DISCLOSURE

27.4.1 Risk management policies

Describe the financial risk management objectives and policies, including the following:
- Policy for hedging each major type of forecasted transaction.
- Price risk (currency, interest rate, and market risk).
- Credit risk.
- Liquidity risk.
- Cash flow risk.

27.4.2 Terms, conditions, and accounting policies

For each class of **financial asset, financial liability,** and **equity instrument**, disclose:
- Information about the extent and nature, including significant terms and conditions that may affect the amount, timing, and certainty of future cash flows, for example:

Principal/notional amounts	Rates or amounts of interest and dividends
Dates of maturities or execution	Collateral held
Early settlement options and periods	Foreign currency information
Conversion options	Covenants, etc.
Amounts and timing of future receipts or payments	

- Accounting policies, including recognition criteria and measurement bases, such as:
  - Methods and assumptions applied in estimating fair value, separately for classes of financial assets and financial liabilities.
  - Whether gains/losses on remeasurement of available-for-sale financial assets are included in profit or loss for the period or recognized directly in equity.
  - Whether 'regular way' financial asset purchases and sales are accounted for at trade date or settlement date (for **each** of the categories of financial assets).

27.4.3 Interest rate risk

For each class of **financial asset** and **financial liability**, disclose:
- Contractual repricing or maturity dates, whichever dates are earlier.
- Effective interest rates.
- Other information about exposure to interest rate risk.

27.4.4 Credit risk

For each class of **financial asset**, disclose:
- The amount that best represents its maximum credit risk exposure **without** taking account of the fair value of collateral.
- Significant concentrations of credit risk.
- Other information about exposure to credit risk.

27.4.5 Fair value

For each class of **financial asset** and **financial liability**, disclose information about fair value:
- Fair value for traded instruments:
  - Asset held or liability to be issued: bid price.
  - Asset to be acquired or liability held: offer price.
- For an instrument not traded, it may be appropriate to disclose a range of amounts.
- When impracticable to determine the fair value reliably, the **fact** is disclosed together with **information** about the principal characteristics of the underlying financial instrument pertinent to its fair value.

27.4.6 Financial assets in excess of fair value

For **financial assets** carried in excess of fair value, disclose:
- Carrying amount and fair value, individually or for appropriate grouping of those assets.
- Reasons for not reducing the carrying amount, including evidence supporting recoverability of the amount.

27.4.7 Hedging

Disclose **separately** for designated fair value hedges, cash flow hedges and hedges of a net investment in a foreign entity:
- Description of the hedge.
- Description of financial instrument(s) designated as hedge, and its fair value(s).
- Nature of the risk being hedged.
- For hedges of forecasted transactions:
  - The period in which it is expected to occur.
  - When it is expected to enter into determination of net profit or loss.
  - Description of any forecasted transaction for which hedge accounting had previously been used but that is no longer expected to occur.
- For gains/losses related to cash flow hedges that have been recognized directly in equity (through the statement of changes in equity):

- Amount recognized in equity.
- Amount removed from equity to net profit or loss for the period.
- Amount removed from equity and allocated to the carrying amount of the asset or liability in a hedged forecasted transaction.

27.4.8 Additional disclosures relating to financial instruments

- For gains/losses from remeasuring available-for-sale financial assets that have been recognized in equity:
    - Amount recognized.
    - Amount removed from equity to net profit or loss for the period.
- Significant items of income, expense, gains, and losses resulting from financial assets and financial liabilities –
    - Interest income and expense shown separately.
    - Realized and unrealized amounts shown separately.
    - Gains and losses from derecognition shown separately from those resulting from fair value adjustments.
    - Amount of interest income accrued on impaired loans shown separately.
- For financial assets measured at amortized cost:
    - A disclosure of that fact.
    - A description of the financial assets.
    - The carrying amount.
    - An explanation of why fair value cannot be measured reliably.
    - A range of estimates within which fair value is highly likely to lie.
    - Disclosure of the following when these assets are sold:
        - The fact.
        - Carrying amount at time of sale.
        - Gain or loss recognized.
- Reason for reclassification of any financial asset to be reported at amortized cost rather than fair value.
- For an impairment loss or reversal of such loss:
    - The nature of the loss.
    - The amount.
- The carrying amount of financial assets pledged as collateral for liabilities and any terms and conditions relating to the pledged assets.
- For securitization or repurchase agreements:
    - Nature and extent of transactions.
    - Description of collateral and quantitative information about key assumptions used in calculating fair values.
    - Whether the financial assets have been derecognized.
- A lender discloses:
    - The fair value of collateral accepted and that it is permitted to sell or repledge in absence of default.
    - The fair value of collateral that it has sold or repledged.
    - Any significant terms and conditions associated with the use of collateral.

> **Appendix III** contains a table that summarizes and combines the disclosure requirements of IAS 1, 30, 32, and 39 **by risk category** for presentation in financial statements of banks and similar institutions.

CASE STUDY

FINANCIAL INSTRUMENTS: DISCLOSURE AND PRESENTATION

The extracts below were taken from the annual reports of several enterprises.
They illustrate some of the disclosure requirements required by IAS 32 and 39.

The following extract from the **Bell Atlantic 1997 Annual Report** illustrates the disclosure of *risk management policies* and *interest rate risk.*

---

10. FINANCIAL INSTRUMENTS

Derivatives

We limit our use of derivatives to managing risk that could negatively impact our financing and operating flexibility, making cash flows more stable over the long run and achieving savings over other means of financing. Our risk management strategy is designed to protect against adverse changes in foreign exchange rates, interest rates and corporate tax rates, and to otherwise facilitate our financing strategies. We use several types of derivatives in managing these risks, including foreign currency forwards and options, interest rate swap agreements, interest rate caps and floors, and basis swap agreements. Derivative agreements are linked to specific liabilities or assets and hedge the related economic exposures. We do not hold derivatives for trading purposes. In 1997 and 1996, we recognized income of $17.3 million and $12.7 million before taxes in our statements of income related to all of our risk management activities.

Interest Rate Risk Management

The following table provides additional information about our interest rate swap agreements, interest rate caps and floors, and basis swap agreements. Certain of our interest rate swap agreements (included below as "Foreign Currency/Interest Rate Swaps") also contain a foreign exchange component which has been described in the "Foreign Exchange Risk Management" section below. We use these interest rate swap agreements to hedge the value of certain international investments. The agreements generally require us to receive payments based on fixed interest rates and make payments based on variable interest rates. The structured note swap agreements convert several structured medium-term notes to conventional fixed rate liabilities while reducing financing costs. The effective fixed interest rates on these notes averaged 6.1 percent and 6.2 percent at December 31, 1997 and 1996. Other interest rate swap agreements, which sometimes incorporate options, and interest rate caps and floors are all used to adjust the interest rate profile of our debt portfolio and allow us to achieve a targeted mix of floating and fixed rate debt. The basis swap agreements hedge a portion of our leveraged lease portfolio against adverse changes in corporate tax rates. The agreements require us to receive payments based on an interest rate index (LIBOR-based) and make payments based on a tax-exempt market index (J.J.Kenney). We account for these basis swap agreements at fair value and recognized income of $4.2 million and $20.2 million in 1997 and 1996 related to mark-to-market adjustments.

The notional amounts shown below are used to calculate interest payments to be exchanged. These amounts are not actually paid or received, nor are they a measure of our potential gains or losses from market risks. They do not represent our exposure in the event of nonperformance by a counterparty or our future cash requirements. Our financial instruments are grouped below based on the nature of the hedging activity.

```
──────── CASE STUDY ────────
         CONTINUED
```

FINANCIAL INSTRUMENTS: DISCLOSURE AND PRESENTATION

On December 31	Notional Amount ($)	Maturities	(Dollars in Millions) Weighted Average Rate	
			Receive (%)	Pay (%)
Interest Rate Swap Agreements:				
Foreign Currency/Interest Rate Swaps				
1997	375.4	1998 – 2002	4.5	6.2
1996	928.4	1997 – 2002	3.3	5.9
Other Interest Rate Swaps				
Pay Fixed				
1997	260.0	1999 – 2005	5.7	5.9
1996	221.2	1997 – 2005	5.7	6.0
Pay Variable				
1997	783.7	1999 – 2006	6.6	6.1
1996	530.7	1997 – 2004	6.5	6.4
Structured Note Swaps:				
1997	60.0	1999		
1996	105.0	1997 – 2004		
Interest Rate Cap/Floor Agreements:				
1997	262.0	1999 – 2001		
1996	140.0	1999 – 2001		
Basic Swap Agreements:				
1997	1,001.0	2003 – 2004		
1996	1,001.0	2003 – 2004		

─────── CASE STUDY ───────

CONTINUED

FINANCIAL INSTRUMENTS: DISCLOSURE AND PRESENTATION

The following extract from the **Chase Manhattan Bank Corporation 1999 Annual Report** illustrates the disclosure of *fair value of financial instruments.*

22 – FAIR VALUE OF FINANCIAL INSTRUMENTS

The fair value of a financial instrument is the current amount that would be exchanged between willing parties (other than in a forced sale or liquidation), and is best evidenced by a quoted market price, if one exists.

Quoted market prices are not available for all of Chase's financial instruments. As a result, the fair values presented are estimates derived using present value or other valuation techniques and may not be indicative of net realizable value. In addition, the calculation of estimated fair value is based on market conditions at a specific point in time and may not be reflective of future fair values.

Certain financial instruments and all nonfinancial instruments are excluded from the scope of SFAS 107. Accordingly, the fair value disclosures required by SFAS 107 provide only a partial estimate of the fair value of Chase. For example, the values associated with the various ongoing businesses that Chase operates are excluded. Chase has developed long-term relationships with its customers through its deposit base and its credit card accounts, commonly referred to as core deposit intangibles and credit card relationships. In the opinion of management, these items in the aggregate add significant value to Chase, but their fair value is not disclosed in this Note.

Fair values among financial institutions are not comparable due to the wide range of permitted valuation techniques and numerous estimates that must be made. This lack of an objective valuation standard introduces a great degree of subjectivity to these derived or estimated fair values. Therefore, readers are cautioned in using this information for purposes of evaluating the financial condition of Chase, compared with other financial institutions.

The following summary presents the methodologies and assumptions used to estimate the fair value of Chase's financial instruments required under the guidelines of SFAS 107.

FINANCIAL ASSETS

Assets for Which Fair Value Approximates Carrying Value: The fair values of certain financial assets carried at cost, including cash and amounts due from banks, deposits with banks, Federal funds sold and securities purchased under resale agreements, due from customers on acceptances, short-term receivables and accrued interest receivable, are considered to approximate their respective carrying values due to their short-term nature and generally negligible credit losses.

Trading Assets: Chase carries trading assets, which include debt and equity instruments as well as the positive fair value on derivative and foreign exchange instruments, at estimated fair value.

————— CASE STUDY —————

CONTINUED

FINANCIAL INSTRUMENTS: DISCLOSURE AND PRESENTATION

Securities: Available-for-sale securities and related derivative contracts are carried at fair value. Held-to-maturity securities are carried at amortized cost. The fair value of actively-traded securities is determined by the secondary market, while the fair value for nonactively traded securities is based on independent broker quotations.

Loans: Loans are valued using methodologies suitable for each type of loan.

The fair value of Chase's commercial loan portfolio is estimated by assessing the two main risk components of the portfolio: credit and interest. The estimated cash flows are adjusted to reflect the inherent credit risk and then are discounted, using a rate appropriate for each maturity that incorporates the effects of interest rate changes. Generally, emerging market loans are valued based on secondary market prices.

For consumer installment loans (including auto financings) and residential mortgages for which market rates for comparable loans are readily available, the fair values are estimated by discounting cash flows, adjusted for prepayments. The discount rates used for consumer installment loans are current rates offered by commercial banks and thrifts. For residential mortgages, secondary market yields for comparable MBSs, adjusted for risk, are used. The fair value of credit card receivables is estimated by discounting expected cash flows. The discount rates used for credit card receivables incorporate the effects of interest rate changes only, since the estimated cash flows are adjusted for credit risk.

Other Assets: This caption consists primarily of private equity investments. Nonpublic investments are carried at cost, which is viewed as an approximation of fair value. The carrying value of nonpublic investments is adjusted for holdings in which a subsequent investment by an unaffiliated party indicates a valuation in excess of cost and for holdings for which evidence of an other-than-temporary decline in value exists.

Public securities held by Chase Capital Partners are valued at quoted market prices (prior to any liquidity discounts) for the purpose of fair value disclosure required by SFAS 107.

FINANCIAL LIABILITIES

Liabilities for Which Fair Value Approximates Carrying Value: SFAS 107 requires that the fair value disclosed for deposit liabilities with no stated maturity (i.e., demand, savings and certain money market deposits) be equal to the carrying value. SFAS 107 does not allow for the recognition of the inherent funding value of these instruments.

The fair value of foreign deposits, Federal funds purchased and securities sold under repurchase agreements, commercial paper, other borrowed funds, acceptances outstanding, accounts payable, and accrued liabilities are considered to approximate their respective carrying values due to their short-term nature.

Domestic Time Deposits: The fair value of time deposits is estimated by discounting cash flows based on contractual maturities at the interest rates for raising funds of similar maturity.

Trading Liabilities: Chase carries trading liabilities, which include securities sold, not yet purchased, structured notes, and derivative and foreign exchange contracts, at estimated fair value.

_____ CASE STUDY _____

CONTINUED

FINANCIAL INSTRUMENTS: DISCLOSURE AND PRESENTATION

Long-Term Debt-Related Instruments: The valuation of long-term debt, including the guaranteed preferred beneficial interests in Chase's junior subordinated deferrable interest debentures, takes into account several factors, including current market interest rates and Chase's credit rating. Quotes are gathered from various investment banking firms for indicative yields for Chase's securities over a range of maturities.

Lending-Related Commitments: Chase has reviewed the unfunded portion of commitments to extend credit as well as standby and other letters of credit, and has determined that the fair value of such financial instruments is not material.

The following table presents the carrying value and estimated fair value of financial assets and liabilities valued under SFAS 107, and certain derivative contracts used for asset/liability activities related to these financial assets and liabilities.

December 31, 1999 (in millions)	Financial Assets/ Financial Liabilities		Derivative Contracts Used for Asset/ Liability Activities			
	Carrying Value[a, b]	Estimated Fair Value[a, b]	Carrying Value[c]	Gross Unrecognized Gains	Gross Unrecognized Losses	Estimated Fair Value[d]
FINANCIAL ASSETS						
Assets for Which Fair Value Approximates Carrying Value	$81,126	$81,126	$4	$15	$(9)	$10
Trading Assets	63,269	63,269	—	—	—	—
Securities Available-for-Sale	60,625	60,625	(22)	—	—	(22)
Securities Held-to-Maturity	888	876	—	—	—	—
Loans, Net of Allowance for Loan Losses	172,702	173,405	(19)	249	(179)	51
Other Assets[e]	8,804	10,168	93	28	(345)	(224)
Total Financial Assets	$387,414	$389,469	$56	$292	$(533)	$(185)
FINANCIAL LIABILITIES						
Liabilities for Which Fair Value Approximates Carrying Value	$292,343	$292,343	$227	$69	$(381)	$(85)
Domestic Time Deposits	30,022	30,207	243	27	(239)	31
Trading Liabilities	38,573	38,573	—	—	—	—
Long-Term Debt-Related Instruments	20,140	19,476	63	79	(213)	(71)
Total Financial Liabilities	$381,078	$380,599	$533	$175	$(833)	$(125)

CASE STUDY

CONTINUED

Financial Instruments: Disclosure and Presentation

December 31, 1998

FINANCIAL ASSETS

Assets for Which Fair Value Approximates Carrying Value	$59,251	$59,251	$41	$70	$(159)	$(48)
Trading Assets	57,692	57,692	—	—	—	—
Securities Available-for-Sale	62,803	62,803	(151)	—	—	(151)
Securities Held-to-Maturity	1,687	1,703	—	—	—	—
Loans, Net of Allowance for Loan Losses	169,202	171,063	90	335	(678)	(253)
Other Assets[e]	5,103	5,444	118	283	(74)	327
Total Financial Assets	**$355,738**	**$357,956**	**$98**	**$688**	**$(911)**	**$(125)**

FINANCIAL LIABILITIES

Liabilities for Which Fair Value Approximates Carrying Value	$247,833	$247,833	$106	$159	$(413)	$(148)
Domestic Time Deposits	35,933	35,746	260	308	(112)	456
Trading Liabilities	38,502	38,502	—	—	—	—
Long-Term Debt-Related Instruments	18,375	18,438	68	430	(31)	467
Total Financial Liabilities	**$340,643**	**$340,519**	**$434**	**$897**	**$(556)**	**$775**

a   Includes the carrying value and estimated fair value of derivative contracts used for asset/liability activities.

b   The carrying value and estimated fair value of daily margin settlements on open futures contracts are primarily included in Other Assets on the balance sheet, except when used in connection with available-for-sale securities, which are carried at fair value and are included in Securities: Available-for-Sale on the balance sheet. Chase uses futures contracts in its asset/liability activities to modify the interest rate characteristics of balance sheet instruments such as available-for-sale securities, loans and deposits. Unrecognized net gains from daily margin settlements on open futures contracts were $22 million at December 31, 1999, in contrast to an unrecognized net loss of $8 million at December 31, 1998.

c   The carrying value of derivatives used for asset/liability activities is recorded as receivables and payables and is primarily included in Other Assets on the balance sheet, except for derivatives used in connection with available-for-sale securities, which are carried at fair value and are included in Securities: Available-for-Sale on the balance sheet.

d   Derivative contracts used for asset/liability activities were valued using market prices or pricing models consistent with methods used by Chase in valuing similar instruments used for trading purposes.

e   At December 31, 1999, deferred gains and losses associated with anticipatory asset/liability transactions were insignificant.

CASE STUDY
CONTINUED

FINANCIAL INSTRUMENTS: DISCLOSURE AND PRESENTATION

The following extract from the **The World Bank 2000 Annual Report** illustrates the disclosure of *credit risk*.

NOTE E – CREDIT RISK

Country Credit Risk: This risk includes potential losses arising from protracted arrears on payments from borrowers. IBRD manages country credit risk through individual country exposure limits according to creditworthiness. These exposure limits are tied to performance on macroeconomic and structural policies. In addition, IBRD establishes absolute limits on the share of outstanding loans to any individual borrower. The country credit risk is further managed by financial incentives such as pricing loans using IBRD's own cost of borrowing and partial interest charge waivers conditioned on timely payment that give borrowers self-interest in IBRD's continued strong intermediation capacity. Collectibility risk is covered by the Accumulated Provision for Loan Losses. IBRD also uses a simulation model to assess the adequacy of its equity including reserves in case a major borrower, or group of borrowers, stops servicing its loans for an extended period of time.

Commercial Credit Risk: For the purpose of risk management, IBRD is party to a variety of financial instruments, certain of which involve elements of credit risk in excess of the amount recorded on the balance sheet. Credit risk exposure represents the maximum potential accounting loss due to possible nonperformance by obligors and counterparties under the terms of the contracts. Additionally, the nature of the instruments involve contract value and notional principal amounts that are not reflected in the basic financial statements. For both on- and off-balance sheet securities, IBRD limits trading to a list of authorized dealers and counterparties. Credit risk is controlled through application of eligibility criteria and volume limits for transactions with individual counterparties and through the use of mark-to-market collateral arrangements for swap transactions. IBRD may require collateral in the form of cash or other approved liquid securities from individual counterparties in order to mitigate its credit exposure. In addition, IBRD has entered into master derivatives agreements which contain legally enforceable close-out netting provisions. These agreements may further reduce the gross credit risk exposure related to the swaps shown below. Credit risk with financial assets subject to a master derivatives arrangement is eliminated *only* to the extent that financial liabilities to the same counterparty are settled after the assets are realized. Because the exposure is affected by each transaction subject to the arrangement, the extent of the reduction in exposure may change substantially within a short period of time following the balance sheet date.

─────── CASE STUDY ───────
CONTINUED

FINANCIAL INSTRUMENTS: DISCLOSURE AND PRESENTATION

The contract value/notional amounts and credit risk exposure, as applicable, of these financial instruments at June 30, 2000 and June 30, 1999 (prior to taking into account any master derivatives or collateral arrangements that have been entered into) are given below:

In millions	*2000*	*1999*
INVESTMENTS - TRADING PORTFOLIO		
Options, futures and forwards		
• Long position	805	3,433
• Short position	1,250	3,653
• Credit exposure due to potential nonperformance by counterparties	*	1
Currency swaps		
• Credit exposure due to potential nonperformance by counterparties	77	182
Cross-currency interest rate swaps		
• Credit exposure due to potential nonperformance by counterparties	306	100
Interest rate swaps		
• Notional principal	13,687	12,924
• Credit exposure due to potential nonperformance by counterparties	3	1
BORROWING PORTFOLIO		
Currency swaps		
• Credit exposure due to potential nonperformance by counterparties	3,863	2,051
Interest rate swaps		
• Notional principal	69,625	55,633
• Credit exposure due to potential nonperformance by counterparties	869	731

* Less than $0.5 million.

CHAPTER 28

EARNINGS PER SHARE (IAS 33)

28.1 PROBLEMS ADDRESSED

Principles for the determination and presentation of earnings per share are prescribed, with a focus on the denominator of the calculation. The standard requires the disclosure of **basic** as well as **diluted** earnings per share.

28.2 SCOPE OF THE STANDARD

This standard applies to entities whose shares are **publicly traded** or in the process of being issued in public securities markets, and other entities that choose to disclose earnings per share. This standard is applicable to consolidated information only if the parent prepares consolidated financial statements.

28.3 ACCOUNTING TREATMENT

28.3.1 An **ordinary share** is an equity instrument subordinate to all other classes of equity instruments. More than one category may be issued by an enterprise.

28.3.2 A **potential ordinary share** is a financial instrument or other contract that may entitle its holder to ordinary shares (e.g., debt or equity instruments that are convertible into ordinary shares, and share warrants and options that give the holder the right to purchase ordinary shares).

28.3.3 **Basic earnings per share (BEPS)** is calculated by dividing the net profit or loss for the period attributable to ordinary shareholders by the weighted average number of ordinary shares.

Basic earnings
- Net profit or loss for the period **after** deducting preference dividends.
- Deduction of preference dividends is:
  - Amount declared for the period on non-cumulative preference shares.
  - Full amount of cumulative preference dividends for the period, whether or not declared.

Weighted number of shares
- The weighted average number of shares outstanding during the period (i.e., the number of ordinary shares outstanding at the beginning of the period, adjusted by those bought back or issued during the period multiplied by a time-weighting factor).
- Contingently issuable shares are considered outstanding and included in the computation of BEPS only from the date when all necessary conditions have been satisfied.
- Adjust the number of shares for **current** and all **previous** periods presented for changes in shares without a corresponding change in resources (e.g., bonus issue and share split).
- Adjust the number of ordinary shares for all periods **prior** to a rights issue that includes a bonus element with the following factor:

Fair value per share immediately prior to the exercise of rights
Theoretical ex-rights fair value per share

28.3.4 Diluted earnings per share (DEPS): The net profit attributable to ordinary shareholders and the weighted average number of shares are adjusted for the effects of all dilutive potential ordinary shares.

Diluted earnings

- The basic earnings are adjusted for **after-tax effects** of the following items associated with dilutive potential ordinary shares:
  - Dividends for the period.
  - Interest for the period.
  - Other changes in income or expense that would result from a conversion of shares (e.g., the savings on interest related to these shares may lead to an increase in the expense relating to a non-discretionary employee profit-sharing plan).

Weighted number of shares

- The weighted average number of shares for BEPS **plus** those to be issued on conversion of all dilutive potential ordinary shares. Potential ordinary shares are treated as dilutive when their conversion would decrease net profit per share from continuing ordinary operations.
- These shares are deemed to have been converted into ordinary shares at the beginning of the period or, if later, the date of the issue of the shares.

28.3.5 Earnings per share amounts should be **restated** as follows:

- If the number of shares outstanding is affected as a result of a capitalization, bonus issue, share split, or a reverse share split, the calculation of BEPS and DEPS should be adjusted retrospectively.
- If these changes occur after balance sheet date but before issue of financial statements, the per share calculations are based on the new number of shares.
- BEPS and DEPS for all periods presented are adjusted for the effect of:
  - Fundamental errors.
  - Changes in accounting policies.
  - Uniting of interests.

28.4   PRESENTATION & DISCLOSURE

28.4.1 PRESENTATION

- BEPS and DEPS are shown with equal prominence on the face of the income statement for **each** class of ordinary share with different rights.
- Even basic and dilutive **losses** per share are shown.

28.4.2 DISCLOSURE

The following should be disclosed:

- Amounts used as numerators for BEPS and DEPS and a reconciliation of those amounts to the net profit or loss for the period.
- Weighted average number of ordinary shares used as the denominator in calculating BEPS and DEPS and a reconciliation of these denominators to each other.
- If an earnings per share figure is disclosed, **in addition** to BEPS and DEPS:
  - Provide a reconciliation of the numerator used with a line item reported in the income statement.
  - Use same denominator as for BEPS.

─────────── CASE STUDY ───────────

EARNINGS PER SHARE

The issued and fully paid share capital of Angli Inc. remained unchanged at the following amounts since the date of incorporation until the financial year ended 31 March 20x4:
- 1,200,000 ordinary shares with no par value.
- 300,000 6% participating preference shares of $1 each.

The corporation has been operating at a profit for a number of years. As a result of a very conservative dividend policy followed by the directors during previous years, there is a large accumulated profit balance on the balance sheet. On 1 July 20x4 the directors decided to issue to all ordinary shareholders, two capitalization shares for every one previously held.

The following abstract was taken from the consolidated income statement for the year ending 31 March 20x5:

	20x5	20x4
	$	$
Profit after tax	400,000	290,000
Minority interest	(30,000)	(20,000)
Net profit from ordinary activities	370,000	270,000
Extraordinary item	–	(10,000)
Net profit for the year	370,000	260,000

The following dividends have been paid/declared at the end of the reported periods:

	20x5	20x4
	$	$
• Ordinary	165,000	120,000
• Preference	34,500	30,000

The participating preference shareholders are entitled to share profits in the same ratio in which they share dividends, after payment of the fixed preference dividend. The shareholders will enjoy the same benefits during liquidation of the company.

The earnings per share (required by **IAS 33**) and the dividends per share (required by **IAS 1**) to be presented in the group financial statements for the year ending 31 March 20x5, is calculated as follows:

	20x5	20x4
EARNINGS PER SHARE:		
Attributable earnings (**Calculation b**) divided by weighted number of shares (**Calculation c**)		
• **Ordinary shares**	320,000	220,000
	3,600,000	3,600,000
	= $0.089	= $0.061
• **Participating preference shares**		
	50,000	40,000
	300,000	300,000
	= $0.167	= $0.133

CASE STUDY

CONTINUED

EARNINGS PER SHARE

	20x5	20x4

DIVIDENDS PER SHARE:

Dividends divided by actual number of shares in issue

- **Ordinary shares**
  (20x4 adjusted for the capitalization issue for the purposes of comparability)

	20x5	20x4
	165,000	120,000
	3,600,000	3,600,000
	= $0.046	= $0.033

- **Preference shares**

	20x5	20x4
	34,5000	30,000
	300,000	300,000
	= $0.115	= $0.10

CALCULATIONS

a. **Percentage of profits attributable to classes of equity shares**

	20x5	20x4
	$	$
Total preference divided	34,500	30,000
Fixed portion (6% x $300,000)	(18,000)	(18,000)
	16,500	12,000
Dividend paid to ordinary shareholders	165,000	120,000

Therefore: The participating preference shareholders share profits in the ratio 1 : 10 with the ordinary shareholders after payment of the fixed preference dividend out of profits.

b. **Earnings per class of share**

	20x5	20x4
	$	$
Net profit for the period	370,000	260,000
Fixed preference dividend	(18,000)	(18,000)
	352,000	242,000
Attributable to ordinary shareholders 10/11	320,000	220,000
Attributable to participating preferance shareholders 1/11	2,000	22,000
Fixed dividend	18,000	18,000
	50,000	40,000

CASE STUDY

CONTINUED

EARNINGS PER SHARE

c.   Weighted number of ordinary shares in issue

	20x5 Shares	20x4 Shares
Balance, 1 April 20x3	1,200,000	1,200,000
Capitalization issue	2,400,000	2,400,000
	3,600,000	3,600,000

CHAPTER 29

INTERIM FINANCIAL REPORTING (IAS 34)

Interim financial information enhances the accuracy for forecasting earnings and share prices. This IAS prescribes the following for interim financial reports:

- Minimum content.
- Principles for recognition and measurement.

This standard applies to all enterprises who are **required** (by law or regulatory bodies) or voluntarily **elect** to publish interim financial reports covering a period shorter than a full financial year (e.g., a semester or quarter).

29.3.1 An interim financial report includes the following (comparative data requirements indicated in parentheses):

- **Condensed balance sheet** (end of interim period and comparative at end of prior full financial year).
- **Condensed income statement(s)** (current interim period and cumulative for current financial year to date, with comparatives for the comparable interim periods of the prior financial year. An enterprise who publishes interim financial reports quarterly would, for example, prepare four income statements in its 3rd quarter, i.e., one for the 9 months cumulatively since the beginning of the year, one for the 3rd quarter only, and comparative income statements for the exact comparable periods of the prior financial year.)
- **Condensed cash flow statement** (cumulative for the current financial year to date and comparative for the comparable interim period of the prior financial year).
- **Condensed changes in equity statement** (cumulative for the current financial year to date and comparative for the comparable interim period of the prior financial year).
- **Selected explanatory notes**.

29.3.2 The **form and content** of an interim financial report is prescribed as follows:

- Include at a **minimum**:
  - Each of the headings and subtotals that were included in the most recent annual financial statements.
  - Selected explanatory notes required by this IAS.
- Basic and diluted earnings per share to be presented on the face of the income statement.
- A parent should prepare the report on a consolidated basis.

29.3.3 In deciding how to recognize, measure, classify, or disclose an item for interim financial reporting purposes, **materiality** should be assessed in relation to the interim period financial data and not the estimated annual data.

29.3.4 An enterprise should apply the same **accounting policies** in its interim financial statements as in its latest annual financial statements, except for accounting policy changes made subsequently.

29.3.5 The frequency of interim reporting (e.g., half-yearly or quarterly) does not affect the **measurement** of an enterprise's annual results. Measurements for interim reporting purposes are therefore made on a year-to-date basis, the so-called **discrete method**.

29.3.6 **Revenues** received seasonally, cyclically, or occasionally (e.g., dividends, royalties, and government grants) should not be anticipated or deferred as of an interim date if anticipation or deferral would not be appropriate at the end of the enterprise's financial year.

29.3.7 **Costs** incurred unevenly during the financial year should be anticipated or deferred for interim reporting purposes only if it is also appropriate to anticipate or defer the costs at the end of the financial year. To illustrate, the cost of a planned major periodic maintenance that is expected to occur late in the year is not anticipated for interim reporting purposes unless the enterprise has a legal or constructive obligation.

29.3.8 While measurements in both annual and interim financial reports are often based on reasonable estimates, the preparation of interim financial reports generally will require a greater **use of estimation methods** than annual financial reports. For example, full stock-taking and valuation procedures may not be required for inventories at interim dates, although it may be done at financial year-end.

29.3.9 A change in accounting policy should be reflected by **restating** the financial statements of prior interim periods of the current financial year **and** the comparable interim periods of prior years in terms of IAS 8 (if practicable).

29.4 DISCLOSURE

29.4.1 INTERIM FINANCIAL REPORT

Selected explanatory notes are intended to provide an update since the last annual financial statements. The following should be included as a **minimum**:
- Statement that accounting policies have been applied consistently or a description of any subsequent changes.
- Explanatory comments about seasonality or cyclicality of operations.
- Nature and amount of items affecting assets, liabilities, equity, net income, or cash flows that are unusual because of their nature, size, or incidence.
- Changes in estimates of amounts reported in prior interim periods of the current year or amounts reported in prior years.
- Changes in outstanding debt or equity, including uncorrected defaults or breaches of a debt covenant.
- Dividends paid.
- Revenue and result of business segments or geographical segments, whichever is the primary format of segment reporting.
- Events occurring after the balance sheet date.
- Purchases or disposals of subsidiaries and long-tern investments, restructurings, and discontinued operations.
- Changes in contingent liabilities or assets.
- The fact that the interim financial report complies with the IAS.

29.4.2 ANNUAL FINANCIAL STATEMENTS

If an estimate of an amount reported in an interim period is changed significantly during the **final interim period** of the financial year but a separate financial report is not published for that final interim period, the nature and amount should be disclosed in a note to the annual financial statements.

CASE STUDY

INTERIM FINANCIAL REPORTING

The following three basic recognition and measurement principles are stated in IAS 34:

A. An enterprise should apply the same accounting policies in its interim financial statements as are applied in its annual financial statements, except for accounting policy changes made after the date of the most recent annual financial statements that are to be reflected in the next annual financial statements. However, the frequency of an enterprise's reporting (annual, half-yearly, or quarterly) should not affect the measurement of its annual results. To achieve that objective, measurements for interim reporting purposes should be made on a year-to-date basis.

B. Revenues that are received seasonally, cyclically, or occasionally within a financial year should not be anticipated or deferred as of an interim date if anticipation or deferral would not be appropriate at the end of the enterprise's financial year.

C. Costs that are incurred unevenly during an enterprise's financial year should be anticipated or deferred for interim reporting purposes if, and only if, it is also appropriate to anticipate or defer that type of cost at the end of the financial year.

The following table illustrates the practical application of the above-mentioned recognition and measurement principles:

PRINCIPLES AND ISSUES	PRACTICAL APPLICATION
A. **Same accounting policies as for annual financial statements** An unexpected devaluation in the reporting currency against other currencies occurred just before the end of the first quarter of the year. This necessitated the recognition of foreign exchange losses on the restatement of unhedged liabilities which are repayable in foreign currencies. Indications are that the reporting currency will regain its position against the other currencies by the end of the second quarter of the year. Management is reluctant to recognise these losses as expenses in the interim financial report and wants to defer it based on the expectation about the reporting currency. They hope that the losses will be neutralized by the end of the next quarter, in order to smooth the earnings rather than recognizing losses in one quarter and profits in the following.	In the annual financial statements, these losses would have to be recognized as expenses in terms of IAS 21, had the devaluation in the currency have happened before balance sheet date. IAS 34, par. 30(b) also states that a cost that does not meet the definition of an asset at the end of an interim period is not deferred on the balance sheet either to await future information as to whether it has met the definition of an asset or to smooth earnings over interim periods within a financial year. The losses will have to be recognized as expenses on a year-to-date basis to achieve the objective of applying the same accounting policies for both the interim and annual financial statements.

CASE STUDY

CONTINUED

INTERIM FINANCIAL REPORTING

PRINCIPLES AND ISSUES	PRACTICAL APPLICATION
B. Deferral of revenues An ice cream manufacturing corporation recently had its shares listed on the local stock exchange. Management is worried about publishing the first quarter's interim results because the enterprise normally earns most of its profits in the third and fourth quarters (during the summer months). Statistics show that the revenue pattern is more or less as follows: 1st quarter = 10% of total annual revenue 2nd quarter = 15% of total annual revenue 3rd quarter = 40% of total annual revenue 4th quarter = 35% of total annual revenue During the first quarter of the current year total revenue amounted to $254,000. However, management plans to report 1/4 of the projected annual revenue in its interim financial report, calculated as follows: $254,000 ÷ 0,10 x 1/4 = $635,000	It is a phenomenon in the business world that some enterprises consistently earn more revenues in certain interim periods of a financial year than in other interim periods, for example, seasonal revenues of retailers. IAS 34 requires that such revenues be recognized when they occur, because anticipation or deferral would not be appropriate at the balance sheet date. Revenue of $254,000 will therefore have to be reported in the first quarter
C. Deferral of expenses An enterprise that reports quarterly has an operating loss carryforward of $10,000 for income tax purposes at the start of the current financial year, for which a deferred tax asset has not been recognized. The enterprise earns $10,000 in the first quarter of the current year and expects to earn $10,000 in each of the three remaining quarters. Excluding the carryforward, the estimated average annual income tax rate is expected to be 40%. Tax expense for the year would be calculated as follows: 40% x (40,000 – 10,000 tax loss) = $12,000 The effective tax rate based on the annual earnings would then be 30% (12,000 ÷ 40,000).	According to IAS 34, par. 3(c) the interim period income tax expense is accrued using the tax rate that would be applicable to expected total annual earnings, that is, the weighted average annual **effective** income tax rate applied to the pre-tax income of the interim period. This is consistent with the basic concept set out in IAS 34, par. 28 that the same accounting recognition and measurement principles should be applied in an interim financial report as are applied in annual financial statements. Income taxes are assessed on an annual basis. Interim period income tax expense is calculated by applying to an interim period's pre-tax income the tax rate that would be applicable to expected total annual earnings, that is, the weighted average annual **effective** income tax rate.

CASE STUDY

CONTINUED

INTERIM FINANCIAL REPORTING

PRINCIPLES AND ISSUES	PRACTICAL APPLICATION
The question is whether the tax charge for interim financial reporting should be based on actual or effective annual rates, which are illustrated below:	This rate would reflect a blend of the progressive tax rate structure expected to be applicable to the full year's earnings.

	Income tax payable	
Quarter	Actual rate	Effective rate
First	nil*	3,000
Second	4,000	3,000
Third	4,000	3,000
Fourth	4,000	3,000
	$12,000	$12,000

* *The full benefit of the tax loss carried forward, is used in the first quarter.*

CHAPTER 30

DISCONTINUING OPERATIONS (IAS 35)

30.1 PROBLEMS ADDRESSED

A basis for segregating information about discontinuing operations from information about continuing operations is established and minimum disclosures are specified.

30.2 SCOPE OF THE STANDARD

This standard applies to all discontinuing operations of all enterprises. It focuses on presentation and disclosure requirements.

30.3 ACCOUNTING TREATMENT

30.3.1 A **discontinuing operation** is a relatively large component.
- that the enterprise, in terms of an overall plan, is either disposing of substantially in its entirety, or is terminating through abandonment, or piecemeal sale,
- which presents a separate major line of business or geographical area of operation, **and**
- that can be distinguished operationally as well as for financial reporting purposes.

30.3.2 A discontinuing operation is based on a single plan within the **control of management** and although discontinuing operations are expected to occur relatively infrequently, income and expense relating to a discontinuing operation should not be presented as an extraordinary item.

30.3.3 The standard requires that disclosure about a discontinuing operation begins as soon as the initial **disclosure event** occurs, i.e., after the occurrence of one of the following, whichever is earlier:
- an enterprise has entered into an agreement to sell substantially all of the assets of the discontinuing operation, or
- its board of directors or other similar governing body has **both** approved a detailed formal plan of discontinuance and made an announcement of the plan.

30.3.4 The standard does not establish specific recognition and measurement criteria. Rather it requires the application of principles set out in other standards. The most relevant standards are those dealing with:
- Provisions and contingencies (IAS 37).
- Impairment of assets (IAS 36).

30.3.5 A discontinuance is completed when the plan is substantially completed or abandoned, though payments from the buyer(s) to the seller may not yet be completed.

30.4 DISCLOSURE

Disclosures are presented separately for **each** discontinuing operation:
Income statement and/or notes
- The amounts of revenue, expenses, and pre-tax profit or loss attributable to the discontinuing operation and the related income tax expense.
- The amount of any gain or loss that is recognized on the disposal of assets or settlement of liabilities attributable to the discontinuing operation and the related income tax expense.

Cash flow statement

- The net cash flows attributable to the operating, investing, and financing activities of the discontinuing operation.

Notes to the financial statements

- A description of the discontinuing operation.
- The business or geographical segment(s) in which it is reported in accordance with IAS 14.
- The date and nature of the initial disclosure event.
- Expected date or period of completion of discontinuance.
- The carrying amounts (as of the balance sheet date) of the total assets and the total liabilities to be disposed of.
- The fact and its effect to be disclosed if an enterprise abandons or withdraws from a plan that was previously reported as a discontinuing operation.
- The net selling prices received or expected from the sale of those net assets for which the enterprise has entered into one or more binding sale agreements, the expected timing thereof, and the carrying amounts of those net assets.
- Financial statements for periods after initial disclosure must update those disclosures, including a description of any significant changes in the amount or timing of cash flows relating to the assets and liabilities to be disposed of or settled and the causes of those changes.
- Comparative information for prior periods, presented in financial statements prepared after initial disclosure, must be restated to segregate the continuing and discontinuing assets, liabilities, income, expenses, and cash flows.
- If an initial disclosure event occurs after the end of an enterprise's financial reporting period but before the financial statements for that period are authorized for issue, those financial statements should include the disclosures above.

Interim financial reports

- Any significant activities or events since the end of the most recent annual reporting report relating to a discontinuing operation and any significant changes in the amount or timing of cash flows relating to the assets and liabilities to be disposed of or settled.

DISCONTINUING OPERATIONS

Outback Inc. specializes in camping and outdoor products and operates in three divisions, namely food, clothes, and equipment. Due to the high cost of local labor, the food division has incurred significant operating losses. Management has decided to close down the division and draw up a plan of discontinuance.

On 1 May 20x2, the board of directors approved the formal plan and it was immediately announced. The following data was obtained from the accounting records for the current and prior year ending 30 June (the numbers are shown in $'000):

	20x2			20x1		
	Food	**Clothes**	**Equip.**	**Food**	**Clothes**	**Equip.**
Revenue	470	1,600	1,540	500	1,270	1,230
Cost of sales	350	500	510	400	400	500
Distribution costs	40	195	178	20	185	130
Administrative expenses	70	325	297	50	310	200
Other operating expenses	30	130	119	20	125	80
Taxation expenses/(benefit)	(6)	137	124	3	80	90

There were no extraordinary items reported in either of the periods.

The following additional costs, which are directly related to the decision to discontinue, are not included in the table above.

Incurred between 1 May and 30 June 20x2

- Severance pay provision $85,000   (These costs are not tax deductible)

Budgeted for the year ending 30 June 20x3

- Other direct costs $73,000
- Severance pay $12,000
- Bad debts $4,000

A proper evaluation of the recoverability of the assets in the food division, in terms of IAS 36, led to the recognition of an impairment loss of $19,000, which is included in the other operating expenses above and are fully tax deductible.

─── CASE STUDY ───
CONTINUED

DISCONTINUING OPERATIONS

Apart from other information required to be disclosed elsewhere in the financial statements, the income statement for the year ending 30 June 20x2 could be presented as follows:

OUTBACK INC.
INCOME STATEMENT FOR THE YEAR ENDED 30 JUNE 20x2

	20x2	20x1
	$'000	$'000
Continuing operations (Clothes & Equipment)		
Revenue	3,140	2,500
Cost of sales	(1,010)	(900)
Gross profit	2,130	1,600
Distribution costs	(373)	(315)
Administrative expenses	(622)	(510)
Other operating expenses	(249)	(205)
Profit before tax	886	570
Income tax expense	(261)	(170)
Net profit for the period	625	400
Discontinuing operation (Food)		
Revenue	470	500
Cost of sales	(350)	(400)
Gross profit	120	100
Distribution costs	(40)	(20)
Administrative expenses	(70)	(50)
Other operating expenses (30 – 19)	(11)	(20)
Impairment loss	(19)	–
Severance pay	(85)	–
(Loss)/Profit before tax	(105)	10
Income tax benefit/(expense)	6	(3)
Net (loss)/profit for the period	(99)	7
Total enterprise net profit for the period	526	407

CHAPTER 31

IMPAIRMENT OF ASSETS (IAS 36)

31.1   PROBLEMS ADDRESSED

The IAS prescribes:

- The procedures that an enterprise applies to ensure that its assets are not overstated; i.e., if its carrying amount exceeds the amount to be recovered through use or sale.
- When an enterprise would account for an identified impairment loss as well as a reversal of an impairment loss.
- Disclosures for impaired assets.

The objective of the standard is to provide detailed guidance on how to exercise **prudence** in measuring the amounts at which assets are shown on the balance sheet.

31.2   SCOPE OF THE STANDARD

This standard covers most assets. It also covers investments in subsidiaries, associates, and joint ventures.

31.3   ACCOUNTING TREATMENT

31.3.1   The recoverable amount of an asset should be estimated if, at the balance sheet date, there is an indication that the asset may be **impaired**. The enterprise should consider, as a minimum, the following:

- **External indicators**, e.g., decline in market value and changes that have an adverse effect on the enterprise.
- **Internal indicators**, e.g., evidence of obsolescence or evidence indicating an asset is performing worse than expected.

31.3.2   The **recoverable amount** of an asset is measured at the **higher** of its net selling price and value in use:

- **Net selling price** is the amount obtainable from the sale of an asset in an arm's length transaction between knowledgeable, willing parties after deducting any direct incremental disposal costs.
- **Value in use** is the present value of estimated future cash flows expected to arise from the continuing use of an asset and its disposal at the end of its useful life. In determining an asset's value in use, an enterprise should use, among other things:
  - cash flow projections (before income taxes and finance costs, but including overheads directly attributable to the use of the asset) based on reasonable and supportable assumptions that reflect the asset in its current condition and represent management's best estimate of the economic conditions that will exist over the remaining useful life of the asset, and
  - a pre-tax discount rate that reflects current market assessments of the time value of money and the risks specific to the asset. The discount rate should not reflect risks for which future cash flows have been adjusted.

31.3.3   An **impairment loss** exists whenever the carrying amount of an asset exceeds its recoverable amount. If either the net selling price or the value in use of an asset exceeds its carrying amount, the asset is not impaired. An impairment loss should be recognized in the **income statement** for assets carried at cost and treated as a **revaluation decrease** for assets carried at a revalued amount (according to IAS 16). After recognition of the impairment loss, the depreciation charge is accordingly adjusted and based on the revised carrying amount.

31.3.4 Recoverable amount should be estimated for an individual asset. If it is not possible to do so, an enterprise determines the recoverable amount for the **cash-generating unit** to which the asset belongs. A cash-generating unit is the smallest identifiable group of assets that generates cash inflows from continuing use, which are largely independent of the cash inflows from other assets or groups of assets.

31.3.5 Principles for **recognizing and measuring** impairment losses for a cash-generating unit are the same as those for an individual asset. In testing a cash-generating unit for impairment, goodwill and corporate assets (such as head office assets) that relate to the cash-generating unit should be considered. If there is an indication that goodwill or a corporate asset may be impaired, the recoverable amount is determined for the cash-generating unit to which they belong. IAS 36 specifies how to determine the carrying amount of a cash-generating unit and how to allocate an impairment loss between the assets of the unit.

31.3.6 An impairment loss recognized in prior years should be **reversed** if, and only if, there has been a change in the estimates used to determine recoverable amount since the last impairment loss was recognized. It is reversed only to the extent that it does not increase the carrying amount of an asset above the carrying amount that would have been determined for the asset (net of amortization or depreciation) had no impairment loss been recognized in prior years. A reversal of an impairment loss should be recognized as **income** for assets carried at cost and treated as a **revaluation increase** for assets carried at revalued amounts.

31.3.7 An impairment loss for goodwill should not be reversed unless:
- the impairment loss was caused by a specific external event of an exceptional nature that is not expected to recur, and
- subsequent external events have reversed the effect of that event.

31.3.8 On first adoption of this standard, it should be applied on a prospective basis, i.e. without restating comparative information.

31.4   DISCLOSURE

The following should be disclosed for **each** class of assets and for **each** reportable segment based on the enterprise's primary format (if IAS 14 is applicable):
- Amount recognized in the income statement for:
  - Impairment losses.
  - Reversals of impairment losses.
- Amount recognized directly in equity for:
  - Impairment losses.
  - Reversals of impairment losses.

If an impairment loss for an individual asset or a cash-generating unit is recognized or reversed and is **material** to the financial statements, disclose the following:
- Events and circumstances that led to the loss recognized or reversed.
- Amount recognized or reversed.
- Details about the nature of the asset or the cash-generating unit and the reportable segments involved.
- Whether the recoverable amount is the net selling price or value in use.
- The basis used to determine the net selling price **or** the discount rate used to determine value in use, and any previous value in use.

If impairment losses recognized (reversed) during the period are **material in aggregate** to the financial statements as a whole, disclose a brief description of:
- The main classes of assets affected.
- The main events and circumstances that led to the losses recognized or reversed.

---- CASE STUDY ----

IMPAIRMENT OF ASSETS

The following information relates to individual equipment items of an enterprise at a balance sheet date:

	Carrying Amount	Net selling price	Value in use
	$	$	$
Item #1	119,000	121,000	114,000
Item #2 (note 1)	237,000	207,000	205,000
Item #3 (note 1)	115,000	117,000	123,000
Item #4	83,000	75,000	79,000
Item #5 (note 2)	31,000	26,000	–

Further information:

1.   Items #2 and #3 are carried at revalued amounts and the revaluation surplus for the items are $12,000 and $6,000 respectively. Both items represent manufacturing equipment.

2.   Item #5 is a bus used for transporting employees in the mornings and evenings. It is not possible to determine the value in use because the bus does not generate cash inflows from continuing use.

The **major** issues related to the possible impairment of the above-mentioned items can be analyzed as follows:

Item #1 — The recoverable amount is defined as the **higher** of an asset's net selling price and its value in use. No impairment loss is recognized because the recoverable amount of $121,000 is higher than the carrying value of $119,000.

Items #2 & #3 — Item #2 is definitely impaired and item #3 is not. The question is how the impairment loss should be recognized. First, it should be calculated as to the difference between $237,000 and the higher of $207,000 and $205,000 = $30,000. According to IAS 36 (par. 59), the loss should be treated as a revaluation decrease.

The question arises whether the revaluation surplus of $6,000 relating to item #3 may also be used because both these items belong to the same class of assets. IAS 36 (par. 60) forbids this treatment; the impairment loss may be recognized against a revaluation surplus only to the extent that the impairment loss does not exceed the amount held in the revaluation surplus for **that same asset**. Accordingly, an amount of $12,000 is recognized against the revaluation surplus relating to item #2 and the resulting $18,000 is recognized as a loss in the income statement.

Item #4 — An impairment loss of $4,000 (the difference between $83,000 and the higher of $75,000 and $79,000) is immediately recognized as an expense in the income statement.

Item #5 — The recoverable amount of the bus cannot be determined in terms of IAS 36 (par. 66), because the asset's value in use cannot be estimated to be close to its net selling price, and it does not generate cash inflows from continuing use that are largely independent of those from other assets.

In this case, management will have to identify the cash-generating unit to which the bus belongs and estimate the recoverable amount of this unit as a whole.

CHAPTER 32

PROVISIONS, CONTINGENT LIABILITIES AND CONTINGENT ASSETS (IAS 37)

32.1 PROBLEMS ADDRESSED

The IAS prescribes the appropriate accounting treatment as well as the disclosure requirements for all provisions, contingent liabilities, and contingent assets to enable users to understand their nature, timing, and amount.

- It sets out the conditions that must be fulfilled for a provision to be recognized. These conditions should assist enterprises to achieve **consistency** and **comparability** in their treatment of provisions, such as decommissioning and other environmental costs, restructurings, and year 2000 costs.
- It guides the preparers of financial statements to decide when they should, in respect of a specific obligation:
  - provide for it (record),
  - disclose information only, or
  - disclose nothing.

32.2 SCOPE OF THE STANDARD

The standard is applicable to all enterprises in accounting for provisions and contingent liabilities/assets, except those resulting from:

- financial instruments carried at fair value,
- executory contracts (e.g., contracts under which both parties have partially performed their obligations to an equal extent),
- insurance contracts with policy holders, and
- events or transactions covered by another IAS (e.g., income taxes and lease obligations).

32.3 ACCOUNTING TREATMENT

32.3.1 The standard distinguishes between other liabilities, provisions, and contingent liabilities as follows:

- A **provision** is a liability of uncertain **timing** or **amount**.
- A **liability** is a **present obligation** of the enterprise arising from past events, the settlement of which is expected to result in an outflow from the enterprise of resources embodying economic benefits, in terms of the Framework (see paragraph 2.3.6).
- A **contingent liability** is either:
  - a **possible obligation**, as it has yet to be confirmed whether the enterprise has a present obligation that could lead to an outflow of resources embodying economic benefits, or
  - a **present obligation** that does not meet the recognition criteria, either because it is not probable that an outflow of resources embodying economic benefits will be required to settle the obligation, or a sufficiently reliable estimate of the amount of the obligation cannot be made.

32.3.2 Provisions can be distinguished from other liabilities such as trade payables and accruals because there is uncertainty about the **timing** or **amount** of the future expenditure required in settlement.

32.3.3 Generally, all provisions are contingent because they are uncertain in timing or amount. However, within this standard the term 'contingent' is used for liabilities and assets that are **not recognized** because:

- their existence will be confirmed by uncontrollable and uncertain future events(s), or
- they do not meet the recognition criteria.

PROVISIONS

32.3.4 A provision should be recognized only when:

- an enterprise has a present obligation (legal or constructive) as a result of a past event (obligating event),
- it is probable that an outflow of resources embodying economic benefits will be required to settle the obligation, and
- a reliable estimate can been made of the amount of the obligation.

32.3.5 In rare cases (e.g., in a law suit), it may not be clear whether an enterprise has a present obligation. In these cases, a past event is deemed to give rise to a present obligation if it is more likely than not that a present obligation exists at balance sheet date.

32.3.6 A **legal** obligation normally arises from a contract or legislation. A **constructive** obligation arises only when **both** of the following conditions are present:

- The enterprise has indicated to other parties, by an established pattern of past practice, published policies or a sufficiently specific current statement, that it will accept certain responsibilities.
- As a result, the enterprise has created a valid expectation on the part of those other parties that it will discharge those responsibilities.

32.3.7 The amount recognized as a provision should be the best estimate of the expenditure required to settle the present obligation at the balance sheet date.

32.3.8 Some or all of the expenditure required to settle a provision may be expected to be reimbursed by another party (e.g., through insurance claims, indemnity clauses, or supplier's warranties). These reimbursement are treated as follows:

- Recognize a reimbursement when it is virtually certain that reimbursement will be received if the enterprise settles the obligation. The amount recognized for the reimbursement should not exceed the amount of the provision.
- Treat the reimbursement as a separate asset.
- The expense relating to a provision may be presented net of the amount recognized for a reimbursement in the income statement.

32.3.9 Provisions should be reviewed at each balance sheet date and adjusted to reflect the current best estimate.

32.3.10 A provision should be used only for expenditures for which the provision was originally recognized.

32.3.11 The IAS provides guidance on the application of the recognition and measurement principles in three specific cases, namely future operating losses, onerous contracts, and restructurings:

- Provisions should not be recognized for **future operating losses**. An expectation of future operating losses is an indication that certain assets of the operation may be impaired — IAS 36, *Impairment of Assets*, would then be applicable.

- The present obligation under an **onerous contract** should be recognized and measured as a provision. An onerous contract is one in which the unavoidable costs of meeting the contract obligations exceed the economic benefits expected to be received under it.

- A **restructuring** is a program planned and controlled by management that materially changes either the scope of business or the manner in which that business is conducted. A provision for restructuring costs is recognized when the normal recognition criteria for provisions are met. A constructive obligation to restructure arises only when an enterprise:
  - has a detailed formal plan for the restructuring, **and**
  - has raised a valid expectation in those affected that it will carry out the restructuring by starting to implement that plan or announcing its main features to those affected by it.

Where a restructuring involves the sale of an operation, no obligation arises for the sale until the enterprise is committed by a binding sale agreement.

CONTINGENT LIABILITIES

32.3.12 An enterprise should not recognize a **contingent liability**. An enterprise should disclose a contingent liability unless the possibility of an outflow of resources embodying economic benefits is remote.

32.3.13 Contingent liabilities are assessed continually to determine whether an outflow of resources embodying economic benefits has become probable. When it becomes probable for an item previously dealt with as a contingent liability, a provision is recognized.

CONTINGENT ASSETS

32.3.14 A **contingent asset** is a possible asset that arises from past events and whose existence will be confirmed only by the occurrence or non-occurrence of one or more uncertain future events not wholly within the control of the enterprise (e.g., an insurance claim that an enterprise is pursuing has an uncertain outcome).

32.3.15 An enterprise should not recognize a contingent asset. A contingent asset should be disclosed where an inflow of economic benefits is probable. When the realization of income is virtually certain, then the related asset is not a contingent asset and its recognition is appropriate in terms of the Framework.

32.4   DISCLOSURE

32.4.1 Provisions

Disclose the following for **each** class separately:

- A detailed itemized reconciliation of the carrying amount at the beginning and end of the accounting period; *comparatives are not required.*

- A brief description of the nature of the obligation and the expected timing of any resulting outflows of economic benefits.

- An indication of the uncertainties about the amount or timing of those outflows.

- The amount of any expected reimbursement, stating the amount of any asset that has been recognized for that expected reimbursement.

32.4.2 Contingent liabilities

Disclose the following for **each** class separately:

- Brief description of the nature.
- Estimate of the financial effect.
- Indication of uncertainties relating to the amount or timing of any outflow.
- The possibility of any reimbursement.

32.4.3 Contingent assets

Disclose the following for **each** class separately:

- Brief description of the nature.
- Estimate of the financial effect.

32.4.4 Exceptions

- Where any information required for contingent liabilities/assets is not disclosed because it is not practicable to do so, it should be stated.
- In extremely rare cases, disclosure of some or all of the information required can be expected to prejudice seriously the position of the enterprise in a dispute with other parties regarding the provision, contingent liability, or contingent asset. In such cases, the information need not be disclosed; however, the general nature of the dispute should be disclosed, along with an explanation why the information had not been disclosed.

DECISION TREE

This diagram summarizes the main requirements of the standard

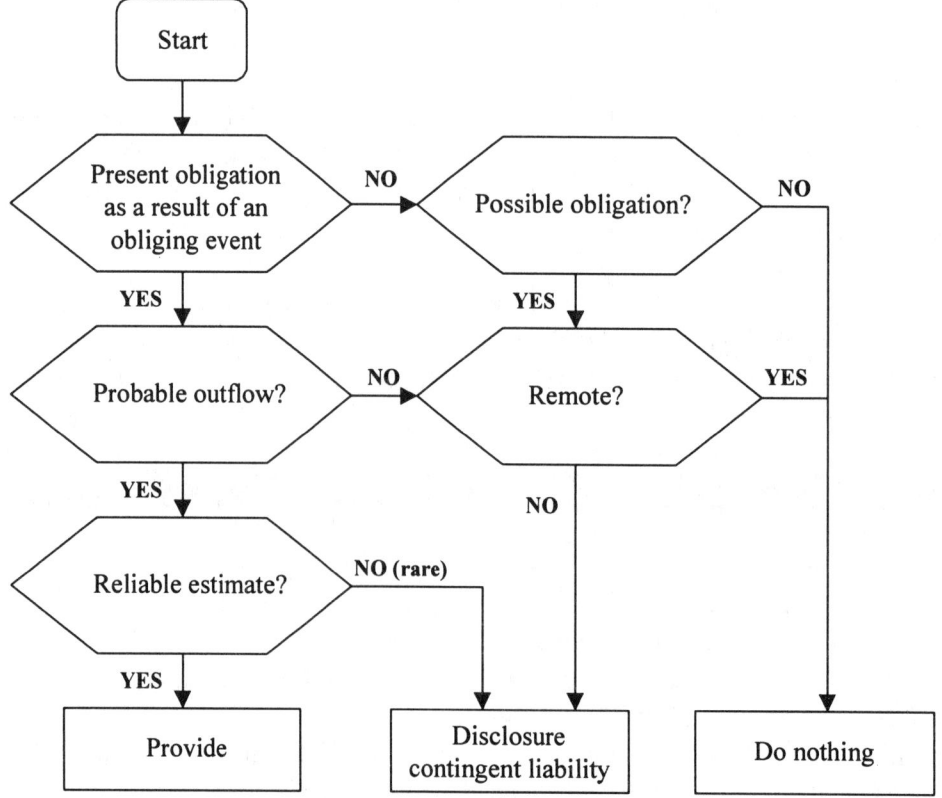

CASE STUDY

PROVISIONS, CONTINGENT LIABILITIES AND CONTINGENT ASSETS

The following scenarios relate to provisions and contingencies:

A.   The Mighty Mouse Trap Company has just started to export mouse traps to the USA. The advertising slogan for the mouse traps is: "A girl's best friend." The Californian Liberation Movement is claiming $800,000 from the company because the advertising slogan allegedly compromises the dignity of women. The company's legal representatives are of the opinion that the success of the claim will depend on the judge who presides over the case. They estimate, however, that there is a 70% probability that the claim will be thrown out and a 30% probability that it will succeed.

B.   Boss Ltd. specializes in the design and manufacture of an exclusive sports car. During the current financial year, 90 sports cars have been completed and sold. During the testing of the sports car, a serious defect was found in its steering mechanism.

All 90 clients were informed by way of a letter of the defect and were required to bring their cars back to have the defect repaired at no charge. All the clients have indicated that this is the only arrangement that they require. The estimated cost of the recall will amount to $900,000.

The manufacturer of the steering mechanism, a listed company with sufficient funds, has accepted responsibility for the defect, and has undertaken to reimburse Boss Ltd. for all costs that it may incur in this regard.

The matters above will be treated as follows for accounting purposes:

A.   **Present obligation as a result of a past event**: The available evidence provided by the experts indicates that it is more likely that no present obligation exists at balance sheet date; there is a 70% probability that the claim will be thrown out. No obligating event has taken place.

Conclusion: No provision is recognized. The matter is disclosed as a contingent liability unless the 30% probability is regarded as being remote.

B.   **Present obligation as a result of a past event**: The constructive obligation derives from the enterprise's letters as well as the valid expectations on the part of the clients that the defects will be repaired.

Outflow of economic benefits: The outflow is beyond any reasonable doubt.

Conclusion: A provision is recognized. However, it is virtually certain that all of the expenditures will be reimbursed by the supplier of the steering mechanism. A separate asset is recognized in the balance sheet. In the income statement, the expense relating to the provision may be shown net of the amount recognized for the reimbursement.

CHAPTER 33

INTANGIBLE ASSETS (IAS 38)

33.1 PROBLEMS ADDRESSED

The following major aspects of accounting for intangible assets are prescribed:

- Recognition as an asset.
- Determination of the carrying amount.
- Determination and the treatment of impairment losses.
- Disclosure requirements.

33.2 SCOPE OF THE STANDARD

IAS 38 applies to all intangible assets that are not specifically dealt with in another IAS. Examples include brand names, computer software, licenses, franchises, and intangibles under development.

33.3 ACCOUNTING TREATMENT

33.3.1 An intangible asset is an identifiable, non-monetary asset without physical substance, held for use in the production or supply of goods or services, for rental to others, or for administrative purposes. Such an asset is controlled and clearly distinguishable from an enterprise's goodwill.

33.3.2 An intangible asset is recognized as an asset (in terms of the Framework) if:

- it is **probable** that the future economic benefits attributable to the asset will flow to the enterprise, and
- the cost of the asset can be **measured reliably**.

All other expenses related to intangible assets are expensed (e.g., research, training, advertising, and start-up costs).

33.3.3 Internally generated goodwill, brands, mastheads, publishing titles, customer lists and items similar in substance should not be recognized as assets.

33.3.4 On **initial** measurement an intangible asset is recognized at **cost** whether it is acquired externally or generated internally. Subsequent expenditure on intangibles are recognized as expenses if it restores the performance standard. These expenditures are capitalized when it is probable that economic benefits in excess of original standard of performance will flow to the enterprise.

33.3.5 Intangible assets may **subsequently** be recorded at either of the following bases:

- Costs less accumulated amortization; i.e., carrying amount/book value (**benchmark treatment**), subject to a write-down to recoverable amount for an impairment loss.
- Revalued amount (**allowed alternative**), being its fair value less accumulated amortization, subject to a write-down to recoverable amount for an impairment loss.

33.3.6 For any internal project to create an intangible asset, the research phase and development phase should be distinguished from one another. Research expenditure is treated as an expense. Development expenditure is recognized as an intangible asset if **all** of the following can be demonstrated:

- The technical feasibility of completing the intangible asset so that it will be available for use or sale.
- The intention to complete the intangible asset and use or sell it.
- The ability to use or sell the intangible asset.
- How the intangible asset will generate probable future economic benefits.
- The availability of adequate technical, financial, and other resources to complete the development and to use or sell the intangible asset.
- The ability to measure the expenditure.

33.3.7 An intangible asset is amortized on a systematic basis over the best estimate of its useful life. There is a rebuttable presumption that the useful life of an intangible asset will not exceed 20 years from the date when the asset is available for use.

33.3.8 The amortization method used should reflect the pattern in which the asset's economic benefits are consumed by the enterprise. If that pattern cannot be determined reliably, the straight-line method should be adopted.

33.3.9 If the 20 years presumption is rebutted, the intangible should be tested for impairment annually and the reason(s) for rebutting the presumption is disclosed.

33.3.10 To assess whether an intangible asset may be impaired, an enterprise should apply IAS 36, *Impairment of Assets*. Also, the standard requires an enterprise to estimate the recoverable amount of an intangible asset that is not yet available for use, at least annually.

33.3.11 In the case of a business combination, expenditure on an intangible item that does not meet both the definition and recognition criteria for an intangible asset should form part of the amount attributed to goodwill.

33.3.12 In certain jurisdictions, the annual amortization charge for an intangible asset would differ from the deduction allowed by the taxation authorities. Deferred taxation should therefore be provided on this difference in terms of IAS 12.

33.3.13 The IAS prescribes different transitional provisions based on the manner in which the reporting enterprise has recognized intangibles in the past.

33.4   DISCLOSURE

33.4.1 The disclosure requirements for **each** class of intangible assets, distinguishing between **internally generated** and **other** intangibles, are as follows:

Accounting policies

- Measurement bases.
- Amortization methods.
- Useful lives or amortization rates.

Income statement and notes

- Amortization charge for each class of asset indicating the line item in which it is included.
- Total amount of research and development costs recognized as an expense.

Balance sheet and notes

- Gross carrying amount (book value) less accumulated depreciation for **each** class of asset at the beginning and the end of the period.
- Detailed itemized reconciliation of movements in the carrying amount during the period; *comparatives are not required.*
- If an intangible asset is amortized over more than 20 years, the evidence that rebuts the presumption that the useful life will not exceed 20 years.
- Carrying amount of intangibles pledged as security.
- Carrying amount of intangibles whose title is restricted.
- Capital commitments for the acquisition of intangibles.
- A description, the carrying amount, and remaining amortization period of any intangible that is material to the financial statements of the enterprise as a whole.
- For intangible assets acquired by way of a government grant and initially recognized at fair value:
  - The fair value initially recognized for these assets.
  - Their carrying amount.
  - Whether they are measured at the benchmark or allowed alternative treatment.

33.4.2 Additional disclosures required for revalued amounts are as follows:

- The effective date of the revaluation.
- Carrying amount of **each** class of intangibles had it been carried in the financial statements on the historical cost basis.
- Amount as well as a detailed reconciliation of the balance of the revaluation surplus.
- Any restrictions on the distribution of the revaluation surplus.

CASE STUDY

INTANGIBLE ASSETS

Alpha Inc., a motor vehicle manufacturer, has a research division that worked on the following projects during the year:

Project 1: The design of a steering mechanism that does not operate like the conventional steering wheel, but react to the impulses from the driver's fingers.

Project 2: The design of a welding apparatus that is controlled electronically rather than mechanically.

The following is a summary of the expenses of the particular department:

	General $'000	**Project 1** $'000	**Project 2** $'000
Material and services	128	935	620
Labor			
• Direct labor	–	620	320
• Department head salary	400	–	–
• Administrative personnel	725	–	–
Overheads			
• Direct	–	340	410
• Indirect	270	110	60

The departmental head spent 15% of his time on project 1 and 10% on project 2.

The capitalization of development costs for the book year would be as follows:

$'000

Project 1: The activity is classified as research and all costs are recognized as expenses	–
Project 2: (620 + 320 + 10% x 400 + 410 + 60)	1,450
	1,450

CHAPTER 34

FINANCIAL INSTRUMENTS: RECOGNITION AND MEASUREMENT (IAS 39)

IAS 32 and 39 were issued as separate standards but are applied in practice as a unit because they deal with exactly the same accounting phenomenon. IAS 39, which deals with the Recognition and Measurement issues of financial instruments, also contains some supplementary disclosures to those required by IAS 32. These requirements are included under Chapter 27.

34.1 PROBLEMS ADDRESSED

The standard establishes principles for recognizing, measuring, and disclosing information about financial instruments in the financial statements. IAS 39 significantly increases the use of **fair value** in accounting for financial instruments, particularly on the asset side of the balance sheet.

34.2 SCOPE OF THE STANDARD

IAS 39 should be applied to all financial instruments as per 34.3.6, except:
- Subsidiaries, associates, and joint ventures.
- Rights and obligations under leases.
- Employee benefit plan assets and liabilities.
- Rights/obligations under insurance contracts.
- Equity instruments issued by the reporting entity.
- Financial guarantee contracts related to failure by a debtor to make payments when due.
- Contingent consideration in a business combination.
- Contracts based on physical variables, e.g. climate.

34.3 ACCOUNTING TREATMENT

INITIAL RECOGNITION

34.3.1 All financial assets and financial liabilities (including derivatives) should be recognized when the enterprise becomes a party to the contractual provisions of an instrument. For the purchase or sale of **financial assets** where market convention determines a fixed period between trade and settlement dates, the trade **or** settlement date may be used for recognition (paragraphs 30-31). Interest is not normally accrued between trade and settlement dates (paragraph 32).

DERECOGNITION

34.3.2 A financial asset, or portion thereof, is derecognized when the enterprise loses control of the contractual rights that comprise the financial asset — through realization, expiry, or surrender of those rights.

34.3.3 When a financial asset is derecognized, the difference between the proceeds and the carrying amount is included in the profit or loss for the period. Any prior revaluation surplus/shortfall is also included in the profit or loss for the period. When a part of a financial asset is derecognized, the carrying amount is allocated proportionally to the part sold using fair value at date of sale and the resulting gain or loss is included in the profit or loss for the period.

34.3.4 A financial liability is derecognized when it is extinguished, i.e. when the obligation discharged, cancelled, or expires.

INITIAL MEASUREMENT

34.3.5 Financial assets and financial liabilities are recognized initially at their cost — the fair value of the consideration given or received. Transaction costs as well as certain hedging gains/losses are also included.

SUBSEQUENT MEASUREMENT

Balance sheet

34.3.6 Subsequent measurement of financial assets and liabilities can be summarized as follows:

MEASURE AT FAIR VALUE	MEASURE AT AMORTIZED COST
Financial Assets Derivatives whether stand-alone or imbedded in non-derivative instruments Financial assets held for trading Available-for-sale financial assets Non-derivative instruments (including financial assets) with fair value exposures *hedged* by derivatives	**Financial Assets** Unlisted instruments (fair value not reliably measurable) Held-to-maturity investments Loans and receivables originated by the entity
Financial Liabilities Derivatives Financial liabilities held for trading Non-derivative instruments (including financial liabilities) with fair value exposures *hedged* by derivatives	**Financial Liabilities** All other liabilities

Gains or losses

34.3.7 Gains or losses on remeasurement to fair value of financial assets and financial liabilities are in general included in net profit or loss for the period. However there are **two exceptions to this rule:**
- Gains/losses on an available-for-sale (non-trading) financial asset may also be recognized in equity until it is sold, when the cumulative amount is transferred to net profit or loss for the period.
- When financial assets and financial liabilities (carried at amortized cost) are being hedged by a hedging instrument, special hedging rules in IAS 39 apply.

IMPAIRMENT OF FINANCIAL ASSETS – GAINS OR LOSSES

34.3.8 An enterprise should assess, at each balance sheet date, whether financial assets may be impaired.

34.3.9 All impairment losses are included in net profit or loss for the period irrespective of the category of financial assets. However, when impairment losses occur for available-for-sale financial assets, for which fair value remeasurements are recognized in equity, an amount should be transferred from equity to net profit or loss for the period.

34.3.10 An impairment loss may be reversed in future periods but the reversal may not exceed the amortized cost for those assets that are not remeasured at fair value.

HEDGE ACCOUNTING

34.3.11 Hedging means designating a derivative or non-derivative financial instrument as an offset to the change in fair value or cash flows of a hedged item. A hedging relationship qualifies for special hedge accounting if the following criteria apply:

- At the inception of the hedge there is formal documentation setting out the hedge details.
- The hedge is expected to be highly effective.
- In the case of a forecasted transaction, the transaction must be highly probable.
- The effectiveness of the hedge is reliably measured.
- The hedge was effective throughout the period.

34.3.12 Hedge accounting recognizes symmetrically the offsetting effects on net profit or loss of changes in the fair values of the hedging instrument and the related item being hedged. Hedging relationships are of three types:

- **Fair value hedge**: Hedges the exposure of a recognized asset or liability (e.g., changes in the fair value of fixed rate bonds as a result of changes in market interest rates).
- **Cash flow hedge**: Hedges the exposure of cash flows related to:
  - a recognized asset or liability (e.g., future interest payments on a bond),
  - a forecasted transaction (e.g., an anticipated purchase or sale of inventories), **or**
  - a firm commitment (e.g., a contract entered into to buy or sell an asset at a fixed price in the enterprise's reporting currency).
- **Hedge of a net investment in a foreign entity**: Hedges the exposure related to changes in foreign exchange rates.

34.3.13 For fair value hedges the gain or loss from revaluing the hedging instrument should be recognized in net profit or loss, and the loss or the gain from adjusting the carrying amount of the hedged items should be recognized in net profit or loss. This applies even if the hedged item is accounted for at cost.

34.3.14 The following rules apply to cash flow hedges:

- The portion of the gain or loss on the hedging instrument deemed to be an effective hedge is recognized directly in equity through the changes in equity statement. The ineffective portion is reported in net profit or loss.
- If the hedged firm commitment or forecasted transaction results in the recognition of an asset or liability, the associated gain or loss previously recognized in equity should be removed and entered into the initial measurement of the acquisition cost of the asset or liability.
- For cash flow hedges that do not result in an asset or liability, the gain or loss in equity should be taken to profit or loss when the transaction occurs.

34.3.15 For hedges of a net investment in a foreign entity, the portion of the gain or loss on the hedging instrument deemed to be an effective hedge is recognized directly in equity through the changes in equity statement. The ineffective portion is reported in net profit or loss.

The accounting rules for hedge accounting are summarized in the table on the following page.

Hedge accounting rules

	Recognize in income statement	Recognize directly in equity	Recognize in initial measurement of asset/liability
Fair value hedge	All adjustments on hedging instrument & hedged item		
Cash flow hedge	Gain/loss on ineffective[2] portion of hedging instrument Gain/loss previously recognized in equity when hedge does not result in asset/liability	Gain/loss on the effective[1] portion of hedging instrument	Gain/loss previously recognized in equity
Hedge of net investment in foreign entity	Gain/loss on ineffective[2] portion of hedging instrument	Gain/loss on the effective[1] portion of hedging instrument	

1. A hedge is normally regarded to be highly effective if, at inception **and throughout the life** of the hedge, the enterprise can expect changes in the fair values or cash flows of the hedged item to be almost fully offset by the changes in the hedging instrument, and actual results are in the range of 80% to 125%. For example, if the loss on a financial liability is 56 and the profit on the hedging instrument is 63, the hedge is regarded to be effective: $63 \div 56 = 112.5\%$.

2. An ineffective hedge would be one where actual results of offset are outside the range mentioned above. Further, a hedge would not be fully effective if the hedging instrument and the hedged item are denominated in different currencies and the two do not move in tandem. Also, a hedge of interest rate risk using a derivative would not be fully effective if part of the change in the fair value of the derivative is due to the counterparty's credit risk.

34.4 DISCLOSURE

Refer to Chapter 27.

———— CASE STUDY ————

FINANCIAL INSTRUMENTS: RECOGNITION AND MEASUREMENT

The following example illustrates the accounting treatment of a hedge (refer to the table on the previous page) of the exposure to variability in cash flows (cash flow hedge) that is attributable to a forecasted transaction.

The Milling Co. is reviewing their maize purchases for the coming season. They anticipate purchasing 1,000 tons of maize after two months. Currently, the two-month maize futures are selling at price of $600 per ton, and they will be satisfied with purchasing their maize inventory at this price by the end of May.

As renewed drought is staring the farmers in the face, they are afraid that the maize price might increase. They therefore hedge their anticipated purchase against this possible increase in the maize price by going long (buying) on two-month maize futures at $600 per ton for 1,000 tons. The transaction requires The Milling Co. to pay an initial margin of $30,000 into their margin account. Margin accounts are updated twice every month.

The following market prices are applicable:

Date	Futures price (per ton)
1 April	$600
15 April	$590
30 April	$585
15 May	$605
31 May	$620 (spot)

The maize price in fact did undergo an increase because of the drought, and The Milling Co. purchases the projected 1,000 tons of maize at the market (spot) price of $620 per ton on 31 May.

Calculation of variation margins

15 April (600-590) x 1,000 tons   = $10,000
30 April (590-585) x 1,000 tons   = $5,000
15 May (605-585) x 1,000 tons   = $20,000
31 May (620-605) x 1,000 tons   = $15,000

The accounting entries will be as follows:

1 April

	Dr	Cr
Initial margin account (B/S)	$30,000	
Cash		$30,000

(Settlement of initial margin)

15 April

Hedging reserve (Equity)	10,000	
Cash		10,000

(Account for the loss on the futures contract – cash flow hedge)

CASE STUDY

CONTINUED

FINANCIAL INSTRUMENTS: RECOGNITION AND MEASUREMENT

	Dr	Cr
30 April		
Hedging reserve (Equity)	5,000	
Cash		$5,000
(Account for the loss on the futures contract – cash flow hedge)		

	Dr	Cr
15 May		
Cash	20,000	
Hedging reserve (Equity)		20,000
(Account for the profit on the futures contract – cash flow hedge)		

	Dr	Cr
31 May		
Cash	15,000	
Hedging reserve (Equity)		15,000
(Account for the profit on the futures contract – cash flow hedge)		

	Dr	Cr
31 May		
Inventory	620,000	
Creditor		620,000
(Purchase the inventory at spot – 1,000 tons @ $620 per ton)		

	Dr	Cr
31 May		
Cash	30,000	
Margin account		30,000
(Receive initial margin deposited)		

	Dr	Cr
31 May		
Hedging reserve (Equity)	20,000	
Inventory		20,000
(Remove the gain or loss on the cash flow hedge from equity and adjust the value of the underlying asset recognized)		

It is clear from this example that the value of the inventory is adjusted with the gain on the hedging instrument, resulting in the inventory being accounted for at the hedged price/futures price.

If the futures contract did not expire or was not closed out on 31 May, the gains or losses calculated on the futures contract thereafter would be accounted for in the income statement as the cash flow hedge relationship no longer exists.

CHAPTER 35

INVESTMENT PROPERTY (IAS 40)

35.1 PROBLEMS ADDRESSED

The following major aspects of accounting for investment property are prescribed:
- Classification as investment property.
- Recognition as an asset.
- Determination of the carrying amount at:
  - Initial measurement.
  - Subsequent measurement.
- Disclosure requirements.

35.2 SCOPE OF THE STANDARD

IAS 40 replaces previous requirements in IAS 25. The standard applies to investment property, being property that is held (by the owner or the lessee under a finance lease) to earn rentals, or for capital appreciation, or both. "Property" includes land and buildings or part of a building or both. It **excludes** owner-occupied property (PPE – see IAS 16), property held for sale (Inventory – see IAS 2), property being constructed or developed (Construction Contracts – see IAS 11), property held by a lessee under an operating lease (Leases – see IAS 17), regenerative natural resources (Biological Assets), and mining and exploration activities.

35.3 ACCOUNTING TREATMENT

35.3.1 Judgement is required when an investment is classified as investment property. A good guideline to use is that an investment property should generate cash flows that are largely independent of the other assets held by the enterprise. Enterprises should develop their own criteria to ensure consistent classification between investment and owner-occupied properties.

35.3.2 An investment property is recognized as an asset (in terms of the IAS Framework) if:
- it is **probable** that the future economic benefits attributable to the asset will flow to the enterprise, and
- the cost of the asset can be **measured reliably**.

35.3.3 On **initial measurement** investment property is recognized at its cost, comprising the purchase price and directly attributable transaction costs (e.g., legal services, transfer taxes, and other transaction costs). However, general administrative expenses as well as start-up costs are excluded.

35.3.4 An enterprise may choose to **subsequently** measure all of its investment property, using either of the following:
- **Cost model**: Measures investment property at cost less accumulated depreciation and impairment losses (the benchmark treatment in IAS 16 for PPE).
- **Fair value model**: All investment properties are valued at fair value. Gains and losses from changes in the fair value are recognized in the income statement as they arise. The fair value model differs from the revaluation model in as far as the gains and losses from changes in

156

the value are recognized in the income statement rather than directly in equity.

35.3.5 The following principles are applied to determine the **fair value** for investment property:
- Where an active market on similar property exists, this may be a reliable indicator of fair value, provided the differences in the nature, condition, and location of the properties are considered and amended, where necessary.
- Other more pragmatic valuation approaches are also allowed when an active market is not available.
- In exceptional circumstances, where it is clear when the investment property is first acquired and that the enterprise will not be able to determine its fair value, such property is measured using the benchmark treatment in IAS 16 until its disposal date. The enterprise measures all of its other investment property at fair value.

35.3.6 **Transfers** to or from investment property should be made when there is a change in use. Special provisions apply for determining the carrying value at date of such transfers.

35.3.7 Subsequent expenditures on investment property are recognized as expenses if they restore the performance standard. These expenditures are capitalized when it is probable that economic benefits **in excess** of the original standard of performance will flow to the enterprise.

35.4   DISCLOSURE

The **main** disclosure requirements include:

Accounting policies
- Criteria to distinguish investment property from owner-occupied property.
- Methods and significant assumptions applied in determining **fair value**.
- Extent to which fair value has been determined by an external independent valuer.
- Measurement bases, depreciation methods, and rates for investment property valued according to the **cost model**.
- The existence and amounts of restrictions on the investment property.
- Material contractual obligations to purchase, construct, or develop investment property or for repairs or enhancement to the property.

Income statement and notes
- Rental income.
- Direct operating expenses arising from an investment property that generated rental income.
- Direct operating expenses from an investment property that did not generate rental income.

Balance sheet and notes
- When an enterprise applies the **fair value model**:
  - A detailed reconciliation of movements in the carrying amount during the period.
  - In exceptional cases when an investment property cannot be measured at fair value (because of a lack of fair value) the reconciliation above should be separately disclosed from other investment property shown at fair value.
- When an enterprise applies the **cost model**:
  - All the disclosure requirements of IAS 16 should be furnished.
  - The fair value of investment property is disclosed by way of a note.

DECISION TREE

This diagram summarizes the classification, recognition, and measurement issues of an investment property. The diagram is based on a decision tree adapted from IAS 40.

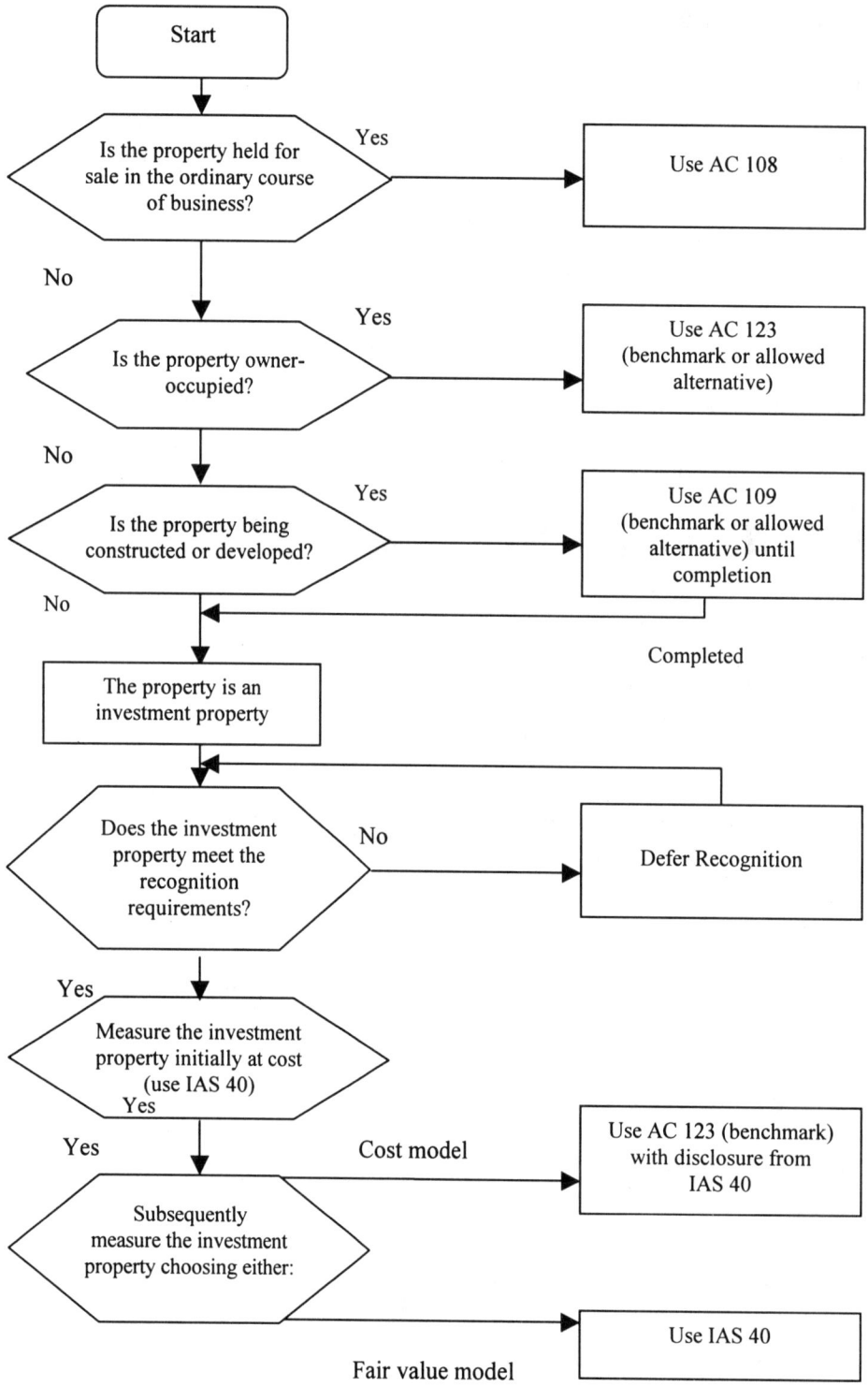

CASE STUDY

INVESTMENT PROPERTY

Matchbox Inc. is a manufacturer of toys for boys. The following information relates to fixed property owned by the company:

	$
Land Erf 181 Hatfield	800,000
Buildings thereon (acquired 30 June 20x0)	2,100,000
Improvements to the building to extend rented floor capacity	400,000
Repairs and maintenance to investment property for the year	50,000
Rentals received for the year	160,000

The property is used as the administrative head office of the company (approximately 6% of floor space). The property can only be sold as a complete unit. The remainder of the building is leased out under operating leases. The company provides lessees with security services.

The company values investment property using the fair value model. On 31 December 20x0, the balance sheet date, Mr. Carmax (a sworn appraiser) valued the property at $3,620,000.

To account for the property in the financial statements of Matchbox Inc. at 31 December 20x0, the property should first be classified as either investment property or owner-occupied property. It is classified as an **investment property** and is accounted for in terms of the fair value model in IAS 40. The motivation is that the portion occupied by the company for administrative purposes is insignificant (6%) and the portions of the property cannot be sold separately. In addition the majority of the floor space of the property is used to generate rental income and the security services rendered to lessee is insignificant.

The accounting treatment and disclosure of the property in the financial statements of Matchbox Inc. are as follows:

BALANCE SHEET AT 31 DECEMBER 20x0

	Note	$
ASSETS		
Non-current assets		
Property, plant, and equipment		Xxx,xxx
Investment property (Calculation a)	4	3,600,000

┌───┐

─── CASE STUDY ───

CONTINUED

INVESTMENT PROPERTY

ACCOUNTING POLICIES

6.   Investment property

Investment property is property held to earn rentals. Investment property is stated at fair value, determined at balance sheet date by an independent sworn appraiser based on market evidence of the most recent prices achieved in arms length transactions of similar properties in the same area.

NOTES TO THE FINANCIAL STATEMENTS

4.   Investment Property

	$
Opening balance	-
Additions	2,900,000
Improvements from subsequent expenditure	400,000
Net gain in fair value adjustments	300,000
Closing balance at fair value	3,600,000

CALCULATION

a.   Carrying amount of investment property

	$
Land	800,000
Building	2,100,000
Improvements to building	400,000
	3,300,000
Fair value	(3,600,000)
Increase in value shown in income statement	(300,000)

└───┘

Appendix I

Currently Valid IASC Standards

As of 31 December 2000

Framework for the Preparation and Presentation of Financial Statements

IAS 1	Presentation of Financial Statements (revised 1997)
IAS 2	Inventories
IAS 3	**No longer effective.** Replaced by IAS 27 and IAS 28
IAS 4	**Withdrawn.** Replaced by IAS 16, IAS 22 and IAS 38
IAS 5	**No longer effective.** Replaced by IAS 1 (revised 1997)
IAS 6	**No longer effective.** Replaced by IAS 15
IAS 7	Cash Flow Statements
IAS 8	Profit or Loss for the Period, Fundamental Errors and Changes in Accounting Policies
IAS 9	**No longer effective.** Replaced by IAS 38
IAS 10	Events After the Balance Sheet Date (revised 1999)
IAS 12	Income Taxes
IAS 13	**No longer effective.** Replaced by IAS 1 (revised 1997)
IAS 14	Segment Reporting
IAS 15	Information Reflecting the Effects of Changing Prices
IAS 16	Property, Plant and Equipment
IAS 17	Leases
IAS 18	Revenue
IAS 19	Employee Benefits
IAS 20	Accounting for Government Grants and Disclosure of Government Assistance
IAS 21	The Effects of Changes in Foreign Exchange Rates
IAS 22	Business Combinations
IAS 23	Borrowing Costs
IAS 24	Related Party Disclosures
IAS 25	**Withdrawn.** Replaced by IAS 40
IAS 26	Accounting and Reporting by Retirement Benefit Plans
IAS 27	Consolidated Financial Statements and Accounting for Investments in Subsidiaries
IAS 28	Accounting for Investments in Associates
IAS 29	Financial Reporting in Hyperinflationary Economies

APPENDIX II

CURRENTLY VALID IASC INTERPRETATIONS

AS OF 31 DECEMBER 2000

SIC–1   Consistency — Different Cost Formulas for Inventories (IAS 2)

SIC–2   Consistency — Capitalization of Borrowing Costs (IAS 23)

SIC–3   Elimination of Unrealized Profits and Losses on Transactions with Associates (IAS 28)

SIC–4   **Withdrawn**

SIC–5   Classification of Financial Instruments — Contingent Settlement Provisions (IAS 32)

SIC–6   Costs of Modifying Existing Software (Framework)

SIC–7   Introduction of the Euro (IAS 21)

SIC–8   First-Time Application of IASs as the Primary Basis of Accounting (IAS 1)

SIC–9   Business Combinations — Classification either as Acquisitions or Unitings of Interests (IAS 22)

SIC–10   Government Assistance — No Specific Relation to Operating Activities (IAS 20)

SIC–11   Foreign Exchange — Capitalization of Losses Resulting from Severe Currency Devaluations (IAS 21)

SIC–12   Consolidation of Special Purpose Entities (IAS 27)

SIC–13   Jointly Controlled Entities — Non-Monetary Contributions by Venturers (IAS 31)

SIC–14   Property, Plant and Equipment — Compensation for the Impairment or Loss of Items (IAS 16)

SIC–15   Operating Leases — Incentives (IAS 17)

SIC–16   Share Capital — Reacquired Own Equity Instruments (Treasury Shares) (IAS 32)

SIC–17   Equity — Costs of an Equity Transaction (IAS 32)

SIC–18   Consistency — Alternative Methods (IAS 1)

SIC–19   **Withdrawn**

SIC–20   Equity Accounting Method — Recognition of Losses (IAS 28)

SIC–21   Income Taxes — Recovery of Revalued Non-Depreciable Assets (IAS 12)

SIC–22   Business Combinations — Subsequent Adjustment of Fair Values and Goodwill Initially Reported (IAS 22)

SIC–23   Property, Plant and Equipment — Major Inspection or Overhaul Costs (IAS 16)

SIC–25   Income Taxes — Changes in the Tax Status of and Enterprise or its Shareholders (IAS 12)

IAS REQUIRED DISCLOSURE IN FINANCIAL STATEMENTS OF BANKS - BY RISK CATEGORY

DISCLOSURE REQUIREMENTS	REFERENCE to IAS
A. MANAGEMENT COMMENTARY Although some banking risks may be reflected in financial statements, users can obtain a better understanding if management provides a *commentary* describing the way it *manages* and *controls* these risks, as follows:	
• Commentary about average interest rates, average interest-earning assets, and average interest-bearing liabilities for a given period.	IAS 30.17
• Information about effective periods and about the way the bank manages and controls risks and exposures associated with the different maturity and interest rate profiles of assets and liabilities.	IAS 30.35
• A discussion of management policies for controlling the risks associated with financial instruments, including policies on matters such as hedging of risk exposures, avoidance of undue concentrations of risk, and requirements for collateral to mitigate credit risks.	IAS 32.42
• Describe the financial risk management objectives and policies, including the policy for hedging each major type of forecasted transaction.	IAS 32.43A
B. FINANCIAL RISKS **1. Balance sheet structure (including off-balance-sheet activities and items)**	
• The basis on which a distinction is made between those transactions and other events that result in the recognition of assets and liabilities and those that only give rise to contingencies and commitments.	IAS 30.8 IAS 1.97
• Terms, conditions, and accounting policies for each class of *financial asset, financial liability,* and *equity instrument,* including information about the extent and nature, including significant terms and conditions, of elements that may effect the amount, timing, and certainty of future cash flows, such as: ▪ principal/notional amounts ▪ dates of maturities or execution ▪ early settlement options and periods ▪ conversion options ▪ amounts and timing of future receipts or payments ▪ rates or amounts of interest and dividends ▪ collateral held ▪ foreign currency information ▪ covenants.	IAS 32.47 IAS 1.97

DISCLOSURE REQUIREMENTS	REFERENCE to IAS

• Accounting policies, including criteria for recognition and measurement bases used, such as:
  ▪ Methods and assumptions applied in estimating fair values, separately for classes of financial assets and financial liabilities.
  ▪ Whether gains/losses on remeasurement of available-for-sale financial assets are included in profit or loss for the period or recognized directly in equity.
  ▪ Whether 'regular way' financial assets purchases and sales are accounted for at trade date or settlement date (for **each** of the categories of financial assets).
	IAS 30.23
	IAS 39.167

• Assets and liabilities may be offset only if:
  ▪ A legal right to do so exists.
  ▪ There is an expectation of realizing an asset or settling a liability on a net basis.
	IAS 30.26

• The following contingencies and commitments are required by IAS 37:
  ▪ The nature and amount of irrevocable commitments to *extend credit*.
  ▪ The nature and amount of contingencies and commitments arising from *off-balance-sheet items*, including:
    ▪ Direct credit substitutes, such as general guarantees of indebtedness, bank acceptance guarantees, and standby letters of credit that serve as financial guarantees for loans and securities.
    ▪ Certain transaction-related contingencies, including performance bonds, bid bonds, warranties, and standby letters of credit related to particular transactions.
    ▪ Short-term, self-liquidating, trade-related contingencies that arise from the movement of goods, such as documentary credits in cases where the underlying shipment is used as security.
    ▪ Sale and repurchase agreements not recognized in the balance sheet.
    ▪ Interest and foreign exchange rate-related items, including swaps, options, and futures.
    ▪ Other commitments, note insurance facilities, and revolving underwriting facilities.
	IAS 37

• The aggregate amount of secured liabilities and the nature and carrying amount of the assets pledged as security.	IAS 30.53

• If the bank is engaged in significant trust activities:
  ▪ The fact to be mentioned.
  ▪ An indication of the extent of those activities.
	IAS 30.55

• Disclose **separately** for designated fair value hedges, cash flow hedges and hedges of a net investment in a foreign entity:
  ▪ Description of the hedge.
  ▪ Description of financial instrument(s) designated as hedge, and its fair value(s).
  ▪ Nature of the risk being hedged.
	IAS 32.91
	IAS 39.169 (b) and (c)

DISCLOSURE REQUIREMENTS	REFERENCE to IAS

- For hedges of forecasted transactions:
  - The period in which it is expected to occur.
  - When it is expected to enter into determination of net profit or loss.
  - Description of any forecasted transaction for which hedge accounting had previously been used but that is no longer expected to occur.
- For gains/losses related to cash flow hedges which have been recognized directly in equity (through the statement of changes in equity):
  - Amount recognized in equity.
  - Amount removed from equity to net profit or loss for the period.
  - Amount removed from equity and allocated to the carrying amount of the asset or liability in a hedged forecasted transaction.

2. Profitability and income statement structure	IAS 30.8
- State the following accounting policies:	IAS 1.97
■ Recognition of the principal types of income.	
■ Determination of charges for general banking risks and the accounting treatment of such charges.	IAS 30.9 and 30.10

- The income statement should group income and expenses by nature and disclose the amounts of the principal types of income and expenses. In addition to the requirements of other IASs, the *income statement* or *the notes* should include the following:
  - interest and similar income
  - interest expense and similar charges
  - dividend income
  - fee and commission income
  - fee and commission expense
  - other operating income
  - general administrative expenses
  - other operating expenses.

- Income and expense items should not be offset except for those related to hedges and to assets and liabilities that have been offset in the balance sheet.	IAS 30.13
- Amounts set aside in respect of general banking risks (including future losses and other unforeseeable risks or contingencies), in addition to those for which accrual must be made in accordance with IAS 37, should be separately disclosed as *appropriations* of retained earnings. Any reductions of such amounts are credited directly to retained earnings.	IAS 30.50

- For gains/losses from remeasuring available-for-sale financial assets, that have been recognized in equity:
   ■ Amount recognized.
   ■ Amount removed from equity to net profit or loss for the period.
	IAS 39.170(a)

- Significant items of income, expense, gain and losses resulting from financial assets and financial liabilities – ■ Interest income and expense shown separately.	IAS 39.170(c)

DISCLOSURE REQUIREMENTS	REFERENCE to IAS
<ul><li>Realized and unrealized amounts shown separately</li><li>Gains and losses from derecognition shown separately from those resulting from fair value adjustments.</li><li>Amount of interest income accrued on impaired loans shown separately.</li></ul> • The nature and amount of any impairment loss or reversal of such loss.	IAS 39.170(f)
3. Solvency risk • For *financial assets* carried in excess of fair value:	IAS 32.88
<ul><li>Carrying amount and fair value, individually or for appropriate grouping of those assets.</li><li>Reasons for not reducing the carrying amount, including evidence supporting recoverability of the amount.</li></ul> *(NOTE: All other items not disclosed at fair value could have a negative impact on solvency risk.)*	
• For financial assets measured at amortized cost: <ul><li>Disclosure of that fact.</li><li>A description of the financial assets.</li><li>The carrying amount.</li><li>An explanation of why fair value cannot be measured reliably.</li><li>A range of estimates within which fair value is highly likely to lie.</li><li>Disclosure of the following when these assets are sold:<ul><li>The fact.</li><li>Carrying amount at time of sale.</li><li>Gain or loss recognized.</li></ul></li></ul>	IAS 39.170(b)
• For securitization or repurchase agreements: <ul><li>Nature and extent of transactions.</li><li>Description of collateral and quantitative information about key assumptions used in calculating fair values.</li><li>Whether the financial assets have been derecognized.</li></ul>	IAS 39.170(d)
• Reason for reclassification of any financial asset to be reported at amortized cost rather than fair value.	IAS 39.170(e)
• The carrying amount of financial assets pledged as collateral for liabilities and any terms and conditions relating to the pledged assets.	IAS 39.170(g)
4. Credit risk • The basis for determining losses on loans and advances and the writing-off of uncollectible loans and advances.	IAS 30.8
• In addition to the requirements of other IASs, the *income statement or the notes* include losses on loans and advances.	IAS 30.10
• In addition to the requirements of other IASs, the *balance sheet or the notes* include the following assets: <ul><li>Placements with and loans and advances to other banks</li><li>Loans and advances to customers.</li></ul>	IAS 30.19

DISCLOSURE REQUIREMENTS	REFERENCE to IAS
• Any significant concentrations of a bank's assets, liabilities, and off-balance-sheet items in terms of geographical areas, customer or industry groups, or other areas of risk concentration.	IAS 30.40
• With regard to losses on loans and advances: 　■ Details of movements in the provision of losses on loans and advances during the period, disclosed separately: 　　▪ Amount recognized as provision for current period. 　　▪ Amount written-off for uncollectibles. 　　▪ Any credited for recovered amounts. 　■ Aggregate amount of the provision for losses on loans and advances on the balance sheet date. 　■ Aggregate amount for loans and advances on which interest is not being accrued and the basis used to determine the carrying amount.	IAS 30.43
• Amounts set aside in respect of losses on loans and advances over and above the normal calculated provision are accounted for as *appropriations* of retained earnings. Any reduction in such amounts should be credited directly to retained earnings and not shown in the income statement.	IAS 30.44
• For related party transactions, the following elements (i.t.o. IAS 24): 　■ Lending policy of the bank. 　■ Amount included in or the proportion of: 　　▪ Loans and advances, deposits and acceptances, and promissory notes. 　　▪ Pprincipal types of income, interest expense, and commissions paid. 　　▪ The expense recognized in the period for losses on loans and advances and the amount of the provision on the balance sheet date. 　　▪ Irrevocable commitments and contingencies arising from off-balance-sheet items.	IAS 30.58
• For each class of *financial asset*: 　■ The amount that best represents its maximum credit risk exposure without taking account of the fair value of collateral. 　■ Significant concentrations of credit risk. 　■ Other information about exposure to credit risk.	IAS 32.66
• A lender discloses: 　■ The fair value of collateral accepted and that it is permitted to sell or repledge in absence of default. 　■ The fair value of collateral that it has sold or repledged. 　■ Significant terms and conditions associated with the use of collateral.	IAS 39.170(h)
*(NOTE: Strict compliance with statutory requirements is not a guarantee of fair presentation. The proper application of the qualitative characteristics of **substance over form** and **prudence** should ensure that information about credit risk is reliable. Both substance and economic reality are important in deter-mining the recoverability of loans and advances. Furthermore, prudence — the inclusion of a degree of caution when making estimates under conditions of uncertainty — should be exercised to ensure that assets and income are not overstated, and liabilities and expenses are not understated.)*	Framework, par .35 and .37

DISCLOSURE REQUIREMENTS	REFERENCE to IAS
5. Liquidity risk • Group assets and liabilities in the balance sheet according to their nature and list them in an order that reflects their relative liquidity.	IAS 30.18

• In addition to the requirements of other IASs, the **balance sheet** or **the notes** include:
  ▪ Assets:
    ▪ cash and balances with the central bank
    ▪ treasury bills and other bills eligible for rediscounting with the central bank
    ▪ government and other securities held for dealing purposes
    ▪ other money market placements.
  ▪ Liabilities:
    ▪ deposits from other banks
    ▪ other money market deposits
    ▪ amounts owed to other depositors
    ▪ certificates of deposits
    ▪ promissory notes and other liabilities evidenced by paper
    ▪ other borrowed funds.
	IAS 30.19

• An analysis and placement of assets and liabilities into relevant **maturity groupings** based on the remaining period between the balance sheet date and the contractual maturity date. Examples of periods used include:
  ▪ up to one month
  ▪ from one month to three months
  ▪ from three months to one year
  ▪ from one year to five years
  ▪ five years or more.
	IAS 30.30 and 30.33

(Maturities can be expressed in terms of the period remaining until the repayment date or from the original period to the repayment date.)	IAS 30.35

6. Interest rate (repricing) risk
• For each class of *financial asset* and *financial liability*:
  ▪ Contractual repricing or maturity dates, whichever dates are earlier.
  ▪ Effective interest rates.
  ▪ Other information about exposure to interest rate risk.
	IAS 32.56

• An analysis and placement of assets and liabilities into relevant **maturity groupings** based on the remaining period to the next date at which interest rates may be changed. Examples of periods used include:
  ▪ up to one month
  ▪ from one month to three months
  ▪ from three months to one year
  ▪ from one year to five years
  ▪ five years or more.
	IAS 30.33 and 30.35

DISCLOSURE REQUIREMENTS	REFERENCE to IAS
7. Market risk	
• The basis for the valuation of investment and dealing securities.	IAS 30.8
• In addition to the requirements of other IASs, the *income statement* or *the notes* include:	IAS 30.10
▪ Gains minus losses arising from dealing securities.	
▪ Gains minus losses arising from investment securities.	
• The following gains and losses are normally reported on a net basis:	IAS 30.15
▪ Disposals and changes in the carrying amount of dealing securities.	
▪ Disposals of investment securities.	
• In addition to the requirements of other IASs, the *balance sheet* or *the notes* include investment securities as a separate class of assets.	IAS 30.19
• The market values of dealing securities and marketable investment securities if they differ from the carrying amounts.	IAS 30.24
• For each class of *financial asset* and *financial liability*, the following information about fair value:	IAS 32.77
▪ Fair value for traded instruments:	
▪ Asset held or liability to be issued: bid price.	
▪ Asset to be acquired or liability held: offer price.	
▪ For an instrument not traded, it may be appropriate to disclose a range of amounts.	
▪ When it is impractical to determine fair value reliably, the *fact* is disclosed together with information about the principal characteristics of the underlying financial instrument that is pertinent to its fair value.	
• For *financial assets* carried in excess of fair value:	IAS 32.88
▪ Carrying amount and fair value, individually or for an appropriate grouping of those assets.	
▪ Reasons for not reducing the carrying amount, including evidence supporting recoverability of the amount.	
(See also section on solvency risk.)	
8. Currency risk	
• In addition to the requirements of other IASs, the *income statement* or *the notes* include:	IAS 30.10
▪ Gains minus losses that arise from dealing in foreign currencies.	
• The following gains and losses are normally reported on a net basis:	IAS 30.15
▪ Dealing in foreign currencies.	
• The amount of significant net foreign currency exposures.	IAS 30.40

BIBLIOGRAPHY

Epstein, B.J. and A.A. Mirza. 1998. *IAS 98 – Interpretation and Application of International Accounting Standards* 1998. New York : John Wiley & Sons.

Hattingh, C.P. 1998. *Financial Accounting Course – One Page Summaries*. Randburg : PC Finance Research CC.

Lewis, R. and D. Pendrill. 1994. *Advanced Financial Accounting, 4th ed.* London : Pitman Publishing.

Oppermann, H.R.B., S.F. Booysen, M. Koen, C.S. Binnekade, and J.G.I. Oberholster. 1997. *Accounting Standards, 7th ed.* Cape Town : Juta.

School of Accountancy. 1995. *The 1995 QE.* Pretoria : University of Pretoria.

Vorster, Q., M. Koen, and C. Koornhof. 2000. *Descriptive Accounting, 5th ed.* Durban : Butterworths.